Student Study Guide

GLENCOE Aviation Technology Series

Aircraft
Electricity & Electronics

Fifth Edition

Thomas K. Eismin

GLENCOE
McGraw-Hill

New York, New York   Columbus, Ohio   Woodland Hills, California   Peoria, Illinois

Student Study Guide for Aircraft Electricity and Electronics, Fifth Edition

ISBN-13: 978-0-02-801860-7
ISBN-10: 0-02-801860-5

Printed in the United States of America.

10 0 QPD/QPD 09

Contents

To the Student   v

Chapter 1. Fundamentals of Electricity   1

Chapter 2. Applications of Ohm's Law   9

Chapter 3. Aircraft Storage Batteries   15

Chapter 4. Electric Wire and Wiring Practices   21

Chapter 5. Alternating Current   27

Chapter 6. Electrical Control Devices   33

Chapter 7. Digital Electronics   43

Chapter 8. Electric Measuring Instruments   51

Chapter 9. Electric Motors   57

Chapter 10. Generators and Related Control Circuits   63

Chapter 11. Alternators, Inverters, and Related Controls   69

Chapter 12. Power Distribution Systems   75

Chapter 13. Design and Maintenance of Aircraft Electrical Systems   83

Chapter 14. Radio Theory   89

Chapter 15. Communication and Navigation Systems   95

Chapter 16. Weather Warning Systems   101

Chapter 17. Electric Instruments and Autoflight Systems   107

Answers   115

To the Student

This Student Study Guide offers the reader a chance to enhance his or her understanding of the materials presented in the textbook *Aircraft Electricity and Electronics,* 5th Edition. The *Study Guide* presents a variety of sample questions and problems that can be used to test the reader's understanding of aircraft electrical system theory, design, and maintenance. The *Study Guide* can also be used to help the student with his or her preparation for the FAA mechanics exams. The materials presented here are directly applicable to current industrial practices and FAA regulations.

The *Study Guide* is divided into 17 chapters. These chapters correspond directly to the 17 chapters of the textbook. Each chapter contains three sections: Study Questions, Multiple-Choice Questions, and Application Questions.

The Study Questions will help the reader to determine what information was retained after reading the text. Any information missed during the initial reading should be reviewed prior to completing the application questions or review exam. The fill-in-the-blank-type study questions are arranged in order as to follow the materials presented in each chapter of the text.

The Multiple-Choice Questions cover all materials contained in a particular chapter in a format similar to those questions used by the FAA. These multiple-choice questions will help the reader determine if he or she should review one or more areas of the text prior to an exam.

The Application Questions are designed to test the reader's knowledge of practical situations dealing with the materials from each chapter.

Reading technical materials is a demanding task. Each chapter of *Aircraft Electricity and Electronics,* 5th Edition, contains an enormous amount of information. In order to understand and retain this information, the student must take sufficient time to study as reading progresses. After a thorough study of each chapter, the student can use the *Study Guide* to test retention of the material. Or, the reader may use the *Study Guide* as a review for exams, such as the FAA mechanics written, oral, and practical tests.

Thomas Eismin

Chapter 1

Name _____

Date _____

STUDY QUESTIONS

1. _____ is merely a special application of electricity wherein precise manipulation of electrons is employed.

2. The _____ describes specifically the internal molecular forces of matter as they pertain to electric power.

3. The smallest particle into which any compound can be divided and still retain its identity is called a

   _____ .

4. An _____ is the smallest possible particle of an element.

5. An _____ is a single substance that cannot be separated into different substances except by nuclear disintegration.

6. A _____ is a chemical combination of two or more different elements.

7. Protons and neutrons form the _____ of an atom.

8. A _____ charge is carried by each proton, no charge is carried by the neutrons, and a

   _____ charge is carried by each electron.

9. When the charge of the nucleus is equal to the combined charges of the electrons, the atom is

   _____ ; but if the atom has a shortage of electrons, it will be

   _____ charged.

10. If an atom has an excess of electrons, it will be _____ charged.

11. A positively charged atom is called a _____ , and a negatively charged atom is called a

    _____ .

12. Certain elements, chiefly metals, are known as _____ because an electric current will flow through them easily.

13. The electrons that move from one atom to another are called _____ .

14. The _____ of any atom is the outermost orbit (shell) of that atom.

15. The electrons in the valence orbit are known as _____ .

16. Materials that have more than half of their valence electrons are called _____ .

17. Materials with exactly half of their valence electrons are _____ .

18. A _____ is the space created by the absence of an electron.

19. The study of the behavior of static electricity is called _____ .

20. The word _____ means stationary, or at rest, and electric charges that are at rest are called

    _____ .

21. The force that is created between two charged bodies is called the _____ .

22. An electric _____ is defined as a flow of electrons through a conductor.

23. One _____ is the rate of flow of one coulomb per second.

24. The term *current* is symbolized by the letter _____ .

25. Current is measured in amperes, which is often abbreviated _____ .

26. The force that causes electrons to flow through a conductor is called _____ .

27. The practical unit for the measurement of emf, or potential difference, is the _____ (V).

28. One _____ is the emf required to cause current to flow at the rate of one ampere through a resistance of one ohm.

29. The term _____ , which is measured in volts, is typically substituted for emf.

30. Voltage is symbolized by the letter _____ , and volts is symbolized by the letter

_____ .

31. _____ is that property of a conductor which tends to hold, or restrict, the flow of an electric current; it is encountered in every circuit.

32. The unit used in electricity to measure resistance is the _____ .

33. Resistance is opposition to current flow and is symbolized by the letter _____ .

34. _____ are materials that have more than four valence electrons.

35. A _____ may be defined as an object that attracts such magnetic substances as iron or steel.

36. A magnetic field is assumed to consist of invisible lines of force that leave the _____ pole of a

magnet and enter the _____ pole.

37. A _____ is one that maintains an almost constant magnetic field without the application of any magnetizing force.

38. A _____ is one found in nature; it is called a _____ , or leading stone.

39. The difference between the geographic and magnetic poles is called _____ .

40. _____ magnetism is the magnetism maintained by a body after it has been magnetized.

41. When the substance is removed from a magnetic field, it will retain its magnetism; hence, it is called a

_____ .

42. The ability of a material to become magnetized is called _____ .

43. A material with _____ permeability is easy to magnetize or demagnetize.

44. A material with _____ permeability is hard to magnetize or demagnetize.

45. Materials with high permeability, such as soft iron, are most useful as _____ magnets.

46. Materials with low permeability, such as alnico, are best suited for _____ magnets.

47. The field of force existing between the poles of a magnet is called a _____ .

48. Magnetic force, which is also called _____ , is said to travel from north to south in invisible lines.

49. The space or substance traversed by magnetic lines of force is called the _____ .

50. The opposition of a material to magnetic flux is called _____ and compares to resistance in an electric circuit.

51. The symbol for reluctance is *R,* and the unit is the _____ .

52. _____ , as the name implies, are produced by using an electric current to create a magnetic field.

53. An electromagnet with a movable core is called a _____ .

54. Electromagnets that contain a fixed core and a pivoting mechanical linkage are called _____ .

55. Relays are usually used for _____ switching applications.

56. The part of a relay attracted by the electromagnet to close the contact points is called the _____ .

57. Friction is a method of producing voltage by simply rubbing two dissimilar materials together. This usually produces

_____ , which is not typically a useful form of power.

58. _____ means electricity created by applying pressure to certain types of crystals.

59. The _____ produces a voltage when light is emitted onto certain substances.

60. Electricity produced by subjecting two dissimilar metals to above normal temperatures is called the

_____ .

61. This combination of two dissimilar metals is called a _____ .

62. _____ is often used to produce electricity for aircraft systems.

63. _____ is the process where by voltage is produced by moving a conductor through a magnetic field.

64. The transfer of electric energy from one circuit to another without the aid of electric connections is called

_____ .

65. When electric energy is transferred by means of a magnetic field, it is called _____ .

66. The two general classifications of electromagnetic induction are _____ and

_____ .

Chapter 1

Name _____

Date _____

MULTIPLE-CHOICE QUESTIONS

Circle the letter of the best answer.

1. A material that can easily be magnetized has which of the following properties?
   a. Residual magnetism
   b. High permeability
   c. Low permeability
   d. Reluctance

2. The potential difference between two conductors that are insulated from each other is measured in
   a. ohms.
   b. volts.
   c. amperes.
   d. coulombs.

3. Materials that have more than half of their valence electrons are called
   a. conductors.
   b. insulators.
   c. semiconductors.
   d. magnets.

4. The potential difference between two conductors that are insulated from each other is measured in
   a. ohms.
   b. volts.
   c. amperes.
   d. coulombs.

5. A material with atoms containing equal numbers of electrons and protons is considered to be
   a. ionized positively.
   b. negatively charged.
   c. ionized negatively.
   d. electrically neutral.

6. Which of the following letters is used to symbolize the term *current*?
   a. *I*
   b. *C*
   c. *A*
   d. *V*

7. Which theory describes specifically the internal molecular forces of matter as they pertain to electric power?
   a. The electron theory
   b. The atomic theory
   c. The molecular theory
   d. The theory of relativity

8. A single substance that cannot be separated into different substances except by nuclear disintegration is called a(n)
   a. compound.
   b. element.
   c. electron.
   d. molecule.

9. Which of the following is another term for *electromotive force?*
   a. Amperage
   b. Voltage
   c. Volts
   d. Resistance

10. Through which material will magnetic lines of force pass most readily?
    a. Copper
    b. Iron
    c. Aluminum
    d. Titanium

Chapter 1

APPLICATION QUESTIONS

1. On the diagram below, draw dotted lines to indicate the magnetic field that surrounds the electromagnet coil.

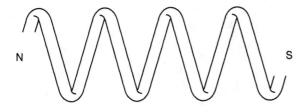

N   S

2. Use the left-hand rule to determine the direction of current flow through the wire in the diagram below.

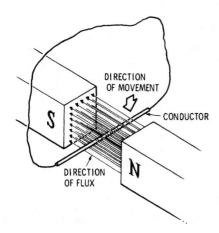

3. Which of the two following diagrams illustrates a solenoid?

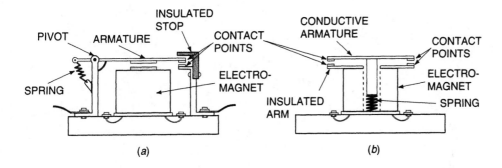

(a)   (b)

Chapter 2

Name _____

Date _____

STUDY QUESTIONS

1. _____ describes the relationships between voltage, amperage, and resistance.

2. In mathematical problems, emf is expressed in volts and the symbol _____ is used to indicate the emf until the actual number of volts is determined.

3. _____ is the symbol for resistance in ohms, and _____ is the symbol for current, or amperage.

4. The letter *I* may be said to represent the _____ of current.

5. The current in an electric circuit is _____ proportional to the emf (voltage) and _____ proportional to the resistance.

6. One _____ causes one ampere to flow through a resistance of one ohm.

7. The equation for Ohm's law is _____ .

8. If the voltage applied to a given circuit is _____ , the current will double.

9. If the resistance is _____ and the voltage remains the same, the current will be reduced by _____ .

10. Power means the rate of doing _____ .

11. One _____ is the power expended when one volt moves one coulomb per second through a conductor.

12. When power is lost in an electric circuit in the form of heat, it is called the _____ .

13. The _____ is a unit of work, or energy, and represents the work done by one watt in one second.

14. To cause a current to flow in a conductor, a difference of _____ must be maintained between the ends of the conductor.

15. In an electric circuit the difference of potential is normally produced by a _____ or a generator.

16. The direction of current flow is from the _____ terminal to the _____ terminal of the battery.

17. The _____ circuit is that part of the complete circuit in which current passes through the airplane structure.

18. A _____ circuit contains only one electron path.

19. In a _____ circuit there are two or more paths for the current, and if the path through one of the units is broken, the other units will continue to function.

20. A circuit that contains electrical units in both parallel and series is called a _____ circuit.

21. In a series circuit the voltage drop across each resistor (load unit) is _____ proportional to the value of the resistor.

22. The current in a parallel circuit _____ proportionately among each resistance (load unit).

23. The total _____ in a parallel circuit is equal to the reciprocal of the sum of the reciprocals of the resistances.

24. The _____ of a number is the quantity 1 divided by that number.

25. In a _____ circuit, the sum of the voltage drops must be equal to the source voltage.

26. In a _____ circuit, the sum of the currents entering a point is equal to the sum of the currents leaving that point.

Chapter 2

MULTIPLE-CHOICE QUESTIONS

Circle the letter of the best answer.

1. How many amperes will a 28-V generator be required to supply to a circuit containing five lamps in parallel, three of which have a resistance of 6 Ω each and two of which have a resistance of 5 Ω each?
   a. 1.11 A
   b. 1 A
   c. 0.9 A
   d. 25.23 A

2. A 24-V source is required to furnish 48 W to a parallel circuit consisting of four resistors of equal value. What is the voltage drop across each resistor?
   a. 12 V
   b. 6 V
   c. 3 V
   d. 24 V

3. Which of the following is Kirchhoff's law for series circuits?
   a. In a series circuit, the algebraic sum of the current flows must be equal to the total current.
   b. In a series circuit, the algebraic sum of the resistances must be equal to the total current deviated by total voltage.
   c. In a series circuit, the total resistance is always less than the smallest resistance of the circuit.
   d. In a series circuit, the algebraic sum of the voltage drops must be equal to the source voltage.

4. The current in a 60-W, 120-V electric lightbulb is
   a. 0.8 A
   b. 2 A
   c. ⅓ A
   d. ½ A

5. A circuit has an applied voltage of 30 V and a load consisting of a 10-Ω resistor in series with a 20-Ω resistor. What is the voltage drop across the 10-Ω resistor?
   a. 15 V
   b. 10 V
   c. 20 V
   d. 30 V

6. Which of the following is correct in reference to electrical resistance?
   a. Two electrical devices will have the same combined resistance connected in series as if connected in parallel.
   b. If one of three bulbs in a parallel lighting circuit is removed, the total circuit resistance becomes greater.
   c. A device with high resistance will use more power than one with low resistance but with the same applied voltage.
   d. A 5-Ω resistor in a 12-V circuit will use less current than a 10-Ω resistor in a 24-V circuit.

7. A 48-V source is required to furnish 192 W to a parallel circuit consisting of three resistors of equal value. What is the value of each resistor?
   a. 36 Ω
   b. 4 Ω
   c. 8 Ω
   d. 12 Ω

8. Which is correct concerning a parallel circuit?
   a. Total resistance will be smaller than the smallest resistance.
   b. Total resistance will decrease when one of the resistances is removed.
   c. Total voltage drop is the same as the total resistance.
   d. Total amperage remains the same, regardless of the resistance.

9. Current in a circuit is directly proportional to which of the following?
   a. Resistance
   b. Voltage
   c. Impedance
   d. Inductance

10. What is the operating resistance of a 30-W lightbulb designed for a 28-V system?
    a. 30 Ω
    b. 1.07 Ω
    c. 26 Ω
    d. 0.93 Ω

11. Which statement is correct when made in reference to a parallel circuit?
   a. The current is equal in all portions of the circuit.
   b. The current in amperes is the product of the emf in volts times the total resistance of the circuit in ohms.
   c. The total current is equal to the sum of the currents through the individual branches of the circuit.
   d. The current in amperes can be found by dividing the emf in volts by the sum of the resistors in ohms.

12. How many watts equals one horsepower?
   a. 244
   b. 550
   c. 746
   d. 0.00134

13. Which statement best describes a series circuit?
   a. A circuit with only one current path
   b. A circuit with a series of many different current paths
   c. A circuit with two or more current paths
   d. A circuit with a maximum of only one load

14. What is the minimum number of resistors needed to create a series-parallel circuit?
   a. 1
   b. 2
   c. 3
   d. 4

15. Which of the following will require the most electric power during operation?
   a. A 12-V motor requiring 8 A
   b. Four 30-W lamps in a 12-V parallel circuit
   c. Two lights requiring 3 A each in a 24-V parallel system
   d. A $\frac{1}{10}$-hp, 24-V motor that is 75 percent efficient

16. Which statement is true concerning resistors connected in parallel?
   a. The total resistance will always be less than the lowest resistance in the parallel group.
   b. The total resistance will never be less than the largest resistance in the parallel group.
   c. The total resistance will always be greater than the lowest resistance in the parallel group.
   d. The total resistance will always be greater than the largest resistance in the parallel group.

17. What unit is used to express electric power?
   a. Coulomb
   b. Volt
   c. Watt
   d. Ampere

18. If three resistors of 3, 5, and 22 Ω are connected in series in a 28-V circuit, how much current will flow through the 3-Ω resistor?
   a. 9.3 A
   b. 1.05 A
   c. 1.03 A
   d. 0.93 A

Chapter 2

APPLICATION QUESTIONS

1. Using Ohm's law, find the voltage drop over R_6, total current, and total resistance for the circuit below.

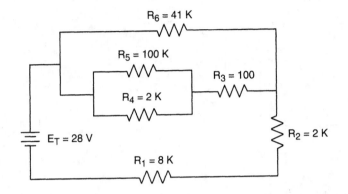

2. For the following series circuit, find the total current flow and the voltage drop over each resistor.

$E_T = 28\ V \qquad R_1 = 4\ K \qquad R_2 = 2\ K \qquad R_3 = 10\ K$

3. If an aircraft alternator has an output of 50 A at 28 V, what is the total power output of the alternator?

4. Find the total current flow for the circuit below.

$R_1 = 200$

$E_T = 40\ V$

$R_2 = 200$

5. Find the total current flow for the circuit below.

$R_1 = 500$

$E_T = 2000\ V$

$R_2 = 100$

$R_3 = 200$

6. If a 28-V signal is applied to a 14K-Ω resistor, how much power will be consumed by the resistor?

7. Find the total current and the total resistance for the circuit below.

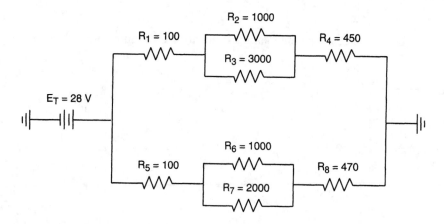

8. Determine the power consumed by a circuit when 400 V is applied to a 500-Ω load.

9. Find both total current and total resistance for the series-parallel circuit below.

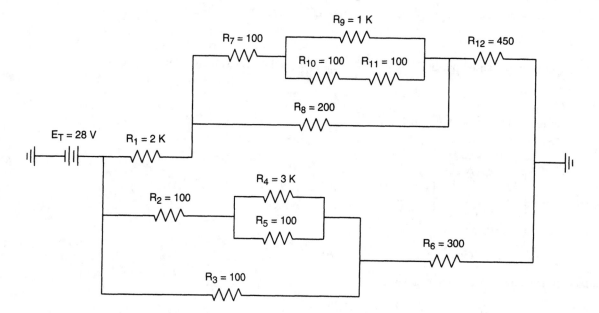

Chapter 3

Name _____

Date _____

STUDY QUESTIONS

1. All battery cells produce _____ voltage.

2. An _____ is technically defined as a compound that, when molten or in solution, conducts electric current and is decomposed by it.

3. The combination of two electrodes surrounded by an electrolyte will form a _____ .

4. An _____ is an atom or molecule that is either positively or negatively charged.

5. A _____ is so called because the electrolyte is in the form of a paste; the cell may therefore be handled without the danger of spillage.

6. A lead-acid secondary cell, such as that employed in storage batteries, develops a voltage of _____ .

7. In a _____ cell, the chemical action that produces the electric current can be reversed.

8. A cell that cannot be recharged is called a _____ cell.

9. Voltaic cells utilizing an alkaline electrolyte are usually termed _____ cells.

10. _____ is a process of heating finely divided metal particles in a mold to approximately melting temperature.

11. Voltage measured when there is no load applied to the battery is called the _____ (OCV).

12. The voltage measured while a load is applied to the battery is called the _____ (CCV).

13. The resistance present inside of a battery while connected to a load is called _____ (IR).

14. A battery's internal resistance always becomes _____ as the battery becomes discharged.

15. A battery of secondary cells is called a _____ battery.

16. Two types of lead-acid batteries currently being used in aviation are (a) the _____ and (b) the _____ battery.

17. On light aircraft, the battery is used for _____ , intermittent loads, and emergency situations.

18. Large turbine-powered aircraft typically use the storage battery only for _____ power.

19. The storage battery on most commercial jets would supply approximately _____ minutes of emergency power in the case of a complete alternator system failure.

20. The positive plates of lead-acid secondary cells are filled with _____ .

21. The negative plates of lead-acid secondary cells are filled with pure spongy _____ .

22. The electrolyte in lead-acid secondary cells consists of a mixture of 30 percent _____ and 70 percent _____ , by volume.

23. Each plate consists of a framework called a _____ .

24. Plate groups are made by joining a number of similar plates to a common _____ .

25. Each plate is made with a lug at the top to which the _____ is fused.

26. The purpose of _____ is to keep the plates separated and thus prevent an internal short circuit.

27. Chemical action takes place _____ as temperature increases.

28. A fully charged battery will not _____ even under the most severe weather conditions.

29. Always wear _____ when servicing a battery.

30. When removing or installing a battery, always remove the _____ lead first and install it last.

31. Do not cause a _____ between the battery terminals.

32. Never service batteries near an _____ .

33. Never jump-start an aircraft from another power source if the airplane's battery is _____ .

34. As a general rule, one should always follow the _____ when servicing an aircraft battery.

35. A _____ is a tool that measures the specific gravity, or density, of a liquid and is used to determine the status of lead-acid battery electrolyte.

36. The _____ of a substance is defined as the ratio of the weight of a given volume of that substance to the weight of an equal volume of pure water at +4°C.

37. The specific gravity of the electrolyte in a lead-acid cell _____ as the charge in the cell decreases.

38. The two general types of charging methods are constant- _____ charging and constant- _____ charging.

39. Batteries should always be charged in a _____ .

40. Always turn off the battery charger before _____ any connections between the battery and the charger.

41. Remove the battery from the aircraft prior to _____ whenever possible.

42. Always take precautions not to spill _____ on skin or clothes; the liquid is very corrosive and will burn.

43. One advantage of the nickel-cadmium cell is that it contains a greater _____ ratio than a lead-acid battery.

44. _____ is a condition where the battery chemicals overheat to such a degree that the battery can be destroyed or even explode.

45. To correct a cell imbalance during reconditioning, a battery is _____ to discharge it to zero capacity and then recharged.

46. _____ is the measure of a battery's total available current.

47. Small batteries are usually rated in _____ because their load drain is usually less than 1 A for several hours.

48. Larger batteries, typical of those found on aircraft, are usually rated in _____ .

Chapter 3

MULTIPLE-CHOICE QUESTIONS

Circle the letter of the best answer.

1. During a load test of a typical 12-V lead-acid battery, if the following readings were obtained when a 150-A load was applied, which would be considered a discharged battery?
   a. Battery 1; CCV = 11.5 V
   b. Battery 2; CCV = 10.0 V
   c. Battery 3; CCV = 8.5 V
   d. Battery 4; CCV = 10.5 V

2. What determines the amount of current that will flow through a battery while it is being charged by a constant-voltage source?
   a. The number of cells in the battery
   b. The total plate area of the battery
   c. The state of charge of the battery
   d. The ampere-hour capacity of the battery

3. When several batteries are being charged at the same time with a constant-current charger,
   a. the batteries can be connected in series with each other and the charger, regardless of their voltage ratings.
   b. all batteries of the same ampere-hour capacity can be connected in series with each other and parallel to the charger.
   c. 24- and 12-V batteries cannot be charged at the same time unless suitable voltage-dropping resistors are placed in the line to the 24-V batteries.
   d. batteries can be connected parallel to the charger, but two or more of the same voltage rating should be connected in series with each other.

4. The electrolyte used in a nickel-cadmium battery is a
   a. potassium hydroxide solution.
   b. hydrochloric acid solution.
   c. sulfuric acid solution.
   d. potassium peroxide solution.

5. Most aircraft storage batteries are rated according to
   a. open-circuit voltage and closed-circuit voltage.
   b. voltage and ampere-hour capacity.
   c. the maximum number of voltamperes (power) the battery can furnish to a load.
   d. battery voltage and volts per cell.

6. Which condition is an indication of improperly torqued cell connectors of a nickel-cadmium battery?
   a. Light spewing at the cell caps
   b. Low temperature in the cells
   c. Toxic and corrosive deposits of potassium carbonate crystals
   d. Heat or burn marks on the connectors and hardware

7. Where is the sediment space located inside of a lead-acid battery?
   a. On top of the cells
   b. On the side of the battery next to the positive terminal
   c. On the side of the battery next to the negative terminal
   d. On the bottom of the battery

8. How many cells are required to produce a 24-V lead-acid battery?
   a. 12
   b. 6
   c. 24
   d. 48

9. The servicing and charging of nickel-cadmium and lead-acid batteries together in the same area is likely to result in
   a. normal battery service life.
   b. thermal runaway in the nickel-cadmium batteries.
   c. increased explosion and fire hazard.
   d. contamination of both types of batteries.

10. The electrolyte of a nickel-cadmium battery is at the lowest level when the battery is
    a. being charged.
    b. fully charged.
    c. in a discharged condition.
    d. under load condition.

11. What may result if water is added to a nickel-cadmium battery when it is not fully charged?
    a. The cell temperatures will run too low for proper output.
    b. The electrolyte will be absorbed by the plates during the charging cycle.
    c. There will be no adverse results, since water may be added anytime.
    d. Excessive spewing will occur during the charging cycle.

12. Batteries that can be discharged and recharged repeatedly are made from what types of cells?
    a. Primary cells
    b. Secondary cells
    c. Carbon cells
    d. Zinc cells

13. When a charging current is applied to a nickel-cadmium battery, the cells emit gas only
    a. toward the end of the charging cycle.
    b. at the start of the charging process.
    c. when the electrolyte level is low.
    d. if they are defective.

14. What part of a nickel-cadmium cell helps to prevent thermal runaway?
    a. The positive plate
    b. The negative plate
    c. The separator
    d. The cell connectors

15. What is the maximum open-circuit voltage value a nickel-cadmium cell will reach immediately after charge?
    a. 1.40 V
    b. 1.28 V
    c. 1.04 V
    d. 1.35 V

16. Which of the following can cause thermal runaway in a nickel-cadmium battery?
    a. Electrical leakage between the cells and the case
    b. A high internal resistance condition
    c. Excessive current draw from the battery
    d. Charging the battery to more than 100 percent of its capacity

17. What is the ampere-hour rating of a storage battery that is designed to deliver 45 A for 2.5 h?
    a. 112.5 Ah
    b. 47.5 Ah
    c. 90.0 Ah
    d. 45.0 Ah

18. For how many hours will a 140-Ah battery deliver 15 A?
    a. 15.0 h
    b. 1.40 h
    c. 9.33 h
    d. 14.0 h

19. Which of the following is true about a recombinant-gas lead-acid cell?
    a. Recombinant-gas batteries are not used for aircraft applications.
    b. Recombinant-gas batteries are sealed cells.
    c. Recombinant-gas batteries are used only on turbine-powered aircraft.
    d. Recombinant-gas batteries produce a higher voltage than other types of lead-acid batteries.

Chapter 3

APPLICATION QUESTIONS

1. With four batteries connected as shown below, what will be the total voltage applied to the load?

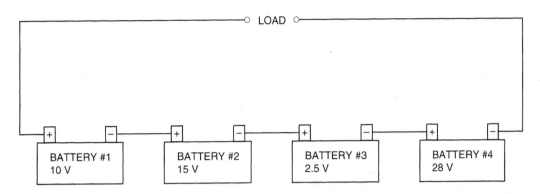

2. With the batteries connected as shown below, what will be the voltage and total amperage available to the load?

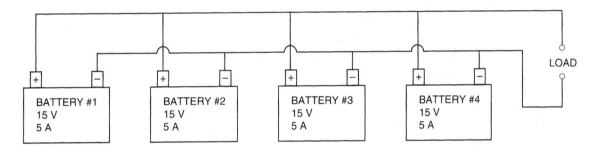

3. Complete the following table, which describes the chemical structure of a lead-acid battery.

	CHARGED STATE	CHEMICAL CHARGE	DISCHARGE
POSITIVE PLATE	PbO_2		$PbSO_4$
NEGATIVE PLATE		GAINS SO_4	$PbSO_4$
ELECTROLYTE	H_2SO_4	LOSES SO_4 GAINS O_2	

Chapter 4

Name _____

Date _____

STUDY QUESTIONS

1. Any type of single conductor surrounded by insulation is usually referred to as a _____ .

2. A _____ is any group of two or more conductors separately insulated and grouped together by an outer sleeve.

3. Some circuits in an airplane require the use of _____ cable to eliminate radio interference or to prevent undesirable voltages from being induced in the circuit.

4. A special application of shielded wire containing a solid copper conductor is called _____ .

5. Coaxial cable is commonly used for connecting an _____ to a radio receiver or transmitter.

6. Whenever possible, wires should be routed in areas of the aircraft that are not subject to extreme

   _____ .

7. The wire used for aircraft electrical installations is sized according to the _____ system.

8. One _____ is equal to the square of the diameter of a wire, in thousandths of an inch.

9. The _____ is the unit of measure for rectangular conductors, such as bus bars or terminal strips.

10. A wire must be able to carry the required _____ without overheating and burning.

11. A wire must carry the required current without producing a _____ greater than what is considered permissible for aircraft circuits.

12. A _____ flow is considered to be any circuit that carries current for a period longer than 2 minutes.

13. _____ circuits carry current for intervals of 2 minutes or less.

14. One special type of wire used exclusively for various digital electronic systems is called

   _____ .

15. When wires or wire bundles are routed through an aircraft without the mechanical protection of conduit, it is called

   _____ .

16. Electrical conduit consists of thin-walled aluminum tubing, braided metal tubing called _____ conduit, and nonmetallic tubing.

17. Nicked and broken strands are _____ for aluminum conductors of any size.

18. _____ are typically considered unsatisfactory for general electrical use in aircraft electrical systems.

19. _____ or a commercially available rosin remover can typically be used to remove flux from soldered joints.

20. The _____ of electric wires may be done if approved for a particular installation.

21. The _____ is a metal tube with a plastic insulator on the outside or a plain metal tube that is covered with a plastic tube after the splice is made.

22. _____ are permitted; however, they are particularly brittle and are not recommended by the FAA.

23. The other type of insulation tubing is called _____ tubing, since it is held in place on the connection through a shrinking process.

24. Special _____ tapes are also approved for certain applications on aircraft terminals and splices.

25. Terminals, nuts, bolts, and washers used with aluminum wiring must be compatible with aluminum to avoid the _____ corrosion that takes place between dissimilar metals when they are in contact.

26. Connectors are used to connect electric and electronic assemblies or _____ such as voltage regulators, flight computers, inverters, and radio equipment.

27. A _____ actually consists of the plug and the receptacle.

28. The plug section generally contains the _____ , and the receptacle contains the _____ .

29. Another type of quick connect/disconnect system used for individual wires is known as the _____ .

30. The process of encapsulating electric wires and components in a plastic material is called _____ .

31. _____ is the process of electrically connecting the various metallic parts of an aircraft or some other flight vehicle so that they will collectively form an integral electric unit.

32. A _____ is a short length of metal braid or metal strip with a terminal at each end for attaching to the structure.

33. _____ is a metallic covering applied to wiring and equipment to eliminate interference caused by stray electromagnetic energy.

34. _____ is caused when electromagnetic fields (radio waves) induce high-frequency (HF) voltages into a wire or component.

35. Protecting one unit from the interference of another is called _____ .

36. The interference caused by high-energy radiated (electromagnetic) fields is known as _____ .

37. To facilitate installation and maintenance, all wiring should be indelibly marked with a _____ .

38. On large, complex aircraft, the wire-numbering system may also contain a _____ to identify which bundle contains a specific wire.

39. To help technicians understand the various current paths and types of wire being used, electrical diagrams, or _____ , are included in the maintenance and installation data for the aircraft electrical systems.

Chapter 4

MULTIPLE-CHOICE QUESTIONS

Name _____

Date _____

Circle the letter of the best answer.

1. What is the maximum number of electric wire terminals that can be installed on one stud?
   a. Four terminals per stud
   b. Three terminals per stud
   c. Two terminals per stud
   d. As many terminals as you can stack on and still have the required number of threads showing through the nut

2. What type of lacing cord installation is recommended for securing large cable bundles?
   a. Single-cord lacing
   b. Double-cord lacing
   c. Triple-cord lacing
   d. Cable tie straps

3. Which of these will cause the resistance of a conductor to decrease?
   a. Decrease the length or the cross-sectional area.
   b. Increase the length or the cross-sectional area.
   c. Decrease the length or increase the cross-sectional area.
   d. Increase the length or decrease the cross-sectional area.

4. What type of wire is typically employed to reduce radio interference produced by certain circuits?
   a. Shielded cable
   b. Coaxial cable
   c. Teflon wire
   d. Stranded wire

5. Aluminum wire must be stripped very carefully because
   a. high resistance will develop in stripping nicks.
   b. low resistance will develop in stripping nicks.
   c. stripping nicks will cause short circuits in wire runs.
   d. individual strands will break easily after being nicked.

6. During the stripping of electric wire, nicked or broken strands are not acceptable for which of the following?
   a. Copper wire of any size
   b. Copper wire size 14 gage or smaller
   c. Any aluminum wire
   d. Aluminum wire size 14 gage or smaller

7. Concerning wire connectors, which type of contact provides the best front-end support?
   a. Front-release contact
   b. Rear-release contact
   c. Pin-type contact
   d. Socket-type contact

8. What is the minimum bend radius for an electric wire bundle?
   a. Ten times the outside diameter of the bundle
   b. Five times the outside diameter of the bundle
   c. Fifteen times the outside diameter of the bundle
   d. Twenty times the diameter of the largest wire in the bundle

9. What protection for wires and cables does conduit provide when used in aircraft installations?
   a. Electromagnetic
   b. Thermal
   c. Mechanical
   d. Structural

10. Which of the following aluminum electric cable sizes would be selected to replace a No. 10 copper electric cable?
    a. No. 4
    b. No. 6
    c. No. 8
    d. No. 10

11. Where electric cables must pass through holes in bulkheads, formers, ribs, fire walls, etc., the wires should be protected from chafing by
    a. wrapping with tape.
    b. using a rubber grommet.
    c. several coats of varnish.
    d. wrapping with plastic.

12. Where are connector housings made from a nylon or plastic material typically used?
    a. In high-vibration areas
    b. On transport-category aircraft
    c. On aluminum wire only
    d. On light aircraft

13. Bonding jumpers should be designed and installed in such a manner that they
    a. are not subjected to flexing by relative motion of the airframe or engine components.
    b. limit the relative motion of the parts to which they are attached by acting as a secondary stop.
    c. provide a low electrical resistance in the ground circuit.
    d. prevent buildup of a static electrical charge between the airframe and the surrounding atmosphere.

14. When electric wiring is installed parallel to a fuel line, the wiring should be
    a. in a metal conduit.
    b. in a vinyl sleeve.
    c. above the fuel line.
    d. below the fuel line.

15. Aircraft electric wire size is measured according to the
    a. Military Specification system.
    b. American Wire Gage system.
    c. Society of Aeronautical Engineers system.
    d. Technical Standard Order system.

16. Copper electric wire for aircraft is coated with tin, silver, or nickel in order to
    a. improve conductivity.
    b. add strength.
    c. prevent oxidation.
    d. prevent crystallization from vibration.

17. What type of wire consists of a twisted pair of wires surrounded by an electrical shielding?
    a. Data bus cable
    b. Coaxial cable
    c. Shielded cable
    d. Aluminum cable

Chapter 4

Name _____

Date _____

APPLICATION QUESTIONS

1. Using the wire selection charts below, determine the wire size needed for a 115-V circuit where a 100-ft wire routed in free air is used to power a 1150-W continuous load.

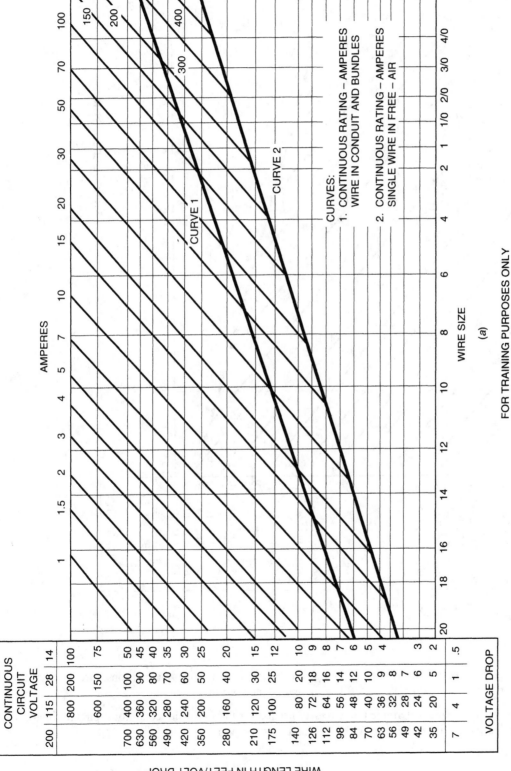

CURVES:
1. CONTINUOUS RATING – AMPERES
   WIRE IN CONDUIT AND BUNDLES
2. CONTINUOUS RATING – AMPERES
   SINGLE WIRE IN FREE – AIR

FOR TRAINING PURPOSES ONLY

WIRE LENGTH IN FEET/VOLT DROP

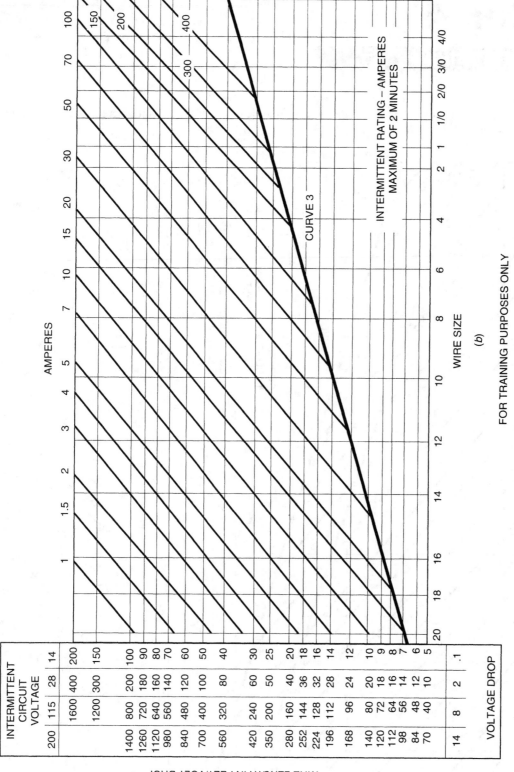

2. Using the wire selection charts, determine the wire size needed for the following conditions: circuit voltage = 28 V, continuous-load current = 70 A, the wire is 30 ft long and is enclosed in a conduit.

3. Using the wire selection charts, determine the wire size needed for the following conditions: circuit voltage = 14 V, intermittent-load current = 100 A, the wire is 12 ft long and is routed in free air.

Chapter 5

Name _____

Date _____

STUDY QUESTIONS

1. _____ current is defined as current that periodically changes direction and continuously changes in magnitude.

2. Values of alternating current and voltage are indicated by a _____ .

3. The number of cycles occurring per second is the _____ of the current and is measured in a unit called the _____ .

4. The word _____ is frequently used in discussing alternating current, and it means one half cycle.

5. The _____ of an alternating current or a voltage is the angular distance it has moved from 0° in a positive direction.

6. The _____ is the difference in degrees of rotation between two alternating currents or voltages, or between a voltage and a current.

7. Three-phase systems are known as _____ .

8. _____ can be defined as the ability to store an electric charge.

9. Most capacitance in a circuit is created by a device called a _____ .

10. The phase shift in capacitive circuits causes the current to _____ the voltage.

11. If capacitance is considered the ability to oppose changes in current flow, then _____ is the actual opposition to current flow in a given ac circuit.

12. The capacitive reactance in a circuit is _____ proportional to the capacitance and the ac frequency.

13. The effect of _____ in ac circuits is exactly opposite to that of capacitance and causes current to lag the voltage.

14. The effect of inductance in an ac circuit is called _____ and is measured in ohms because it "resists" the flow of current in the circuit.

15. The inductive reactance in a circuit is _____ to the inductance of the circuit and the frequency of the alternating current.

16. A circuit containing only resistance is called a _____ .

17. An *RC* circuit contains both resistive units and _____ units.

18. For any circuit that is not purely resistive, the total opposition to current flow is called _____ .

19. _____ is the power consumed by the resistance of an ac circuit.

20. _____ is the power consumed by the entire ac circuit.

21. _____ is a function of the total reactance of a circuit.

22. To distinguish between the types of power, true power is measured in _____ , apparent power is measured in _____ , and reactive power is measured in _____ .

23. _____ is the ratio of true power to apparent power.

24. Modern, large transport-category aircraft of all types employ a _____ ac electrical system.

25. Through the principle of electromagnetic induction, ac voltage can easily be increased or decreased to virtually any desired level through the use of a _____ .

26. An _____ is a device that changes dc voltage to ac voltage.

Chapter 5

Name _____

Date _____

MULTIPLE-CHOICE QUESTIONS

Circle the letter of the best answer.

1. The term that describes the combined resistive forces in an ac circuit is
   a. resistance.
   b. capacitance.
   c. total resistance.
   d. impedance.

2. The power factor in an ac circuit is equal to the _____ of the phase shift angle (Θ).
   a. sine
   b. cosine
   c. tangent
   d. cotangent

3. In an ac circuit with no phase lead or lag, which is true?
   a. Real power is zero.
   b. Reactive power is maximum.
   c. Real power is greater than apparent power.
   d. Real power equals apparent power.

4. Which of the following is a true statement concerning alternating current?
   a. The effective voltage is always less than the peak voltage.
   b. The maximum voltage is always less than the rms voltage.
   c. The rms voltage is always less than the effective voltage.
   d. The peak voltage is always less than the maximum voltage.

5. The opposition offered by a coil to the flow of alternating current is called
   a. conductivity.
   b. impedance.
   c. reluctance.
   d. inductive reactance.

6. An increase in which of the following factors will cause an increase in the inductive reactance of a circuit?
   a. Frequency
   b. Capacitance
   c. Voltage
   d. Resistance

7. When the capacitive reactance in an ac electric circuit is equal to the inductive reactance, the circuit is said to be
   a. in correct voltage phase angle.
   b. in correct current phase angle.
   c. out of phase.
   d. in phase.

8. What is the actual opposition to current flow created by a capacitor in an ac circuit?
   a. Capacitance
   b. Impedance
   c. Capacitive resistance
   d. Capacitive reactance

9. In an ac circuit, the effective voltage
   a. is equal to the maximum instantaneous voltage.
   b. is greater than the maximum instantaneous voltage.
   c. may be greater or less than the maximum instantaneous voltage.
   d. is less than the maximum instantaneous voltage.

10. One megahertz is equal to which of the following?
    a. 1000 Hz
    b. 1,000,000 Hz
    c. 100 Hz
    d. 1,000,000,000 Hz

11. Unless otherwise specified, any values given for current or voltage in an ac circuit are assumed to be
    a. average values.
    b. instantaneous values.
    c. effective values.
    d. maximum values.

12. When power is calculated in a reactive or inductive ac circuit, the true power is
    a. more than the apparent power.
    b. more than the apparent power in a reactive circuit and less than the apparent power in an inductive circuit.
    c. less than the apparent power in a reactive circuit and more than the apparent power in an inductive circuit.
    d. less than the apparent power.

13. When installed in an ac circuit, which of the following components will cause current to lag voltage?
    a. Capacitors
    b. Inductors
    c. Resistors
    d. Transistors

Chapter 5

APPLICATION QUESTIONS

1. Calculate the rms voltage for the ac voltage curve shown below.

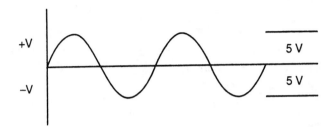

+V

−V

5 V

5 V

2. Determine the frequency of the ac voltage curve shown below.

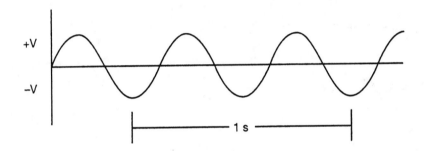

+V

−V

1 s

3. Find the total capacitance of the circuit below.

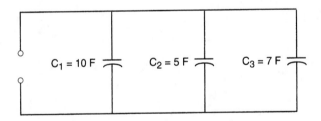

$C_1 = 10$ F $C_2 = 5$ F $C_3 = 7$ F

4. Find the total capacitance of the series circuit below.

$C_1 = 15$ F $C_2 = 10$ F $C_3 = 2$ F

5. Find the total capacitive reactance for the circuit below.

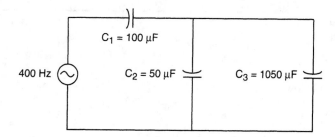

6. Determine the inductive reactance created by a 10-H inductor connected to a 400-Hz voltage.

7. Find the total impedance for the series ac circuit shown below.

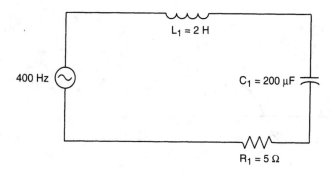

Chapter 6

Name _____

Date _____

STUDY QUESTIONS

1. A _____ can be defined as a device for closing or opening an electric circuit.

2. Electrically operated switches are generally called relays or _____ .

3. The _____ is a multiplier that is used to establish the capacity a switch should have in order to control a particular type of circuit without damage.

4. Spring-loaded switches can be either normally _____ or normally _____ .

5. The contact points of a _____ switch are disconnected (open) until pressure is applied to the switch-actuating mechanism.

6. If pressure is applied to a normally open switch's actuator, the contact points _____ .

7. A _____ switch contains closed contact points when there is no force applied to the switch actuator, and open points when a force is applied.

8. Solenoids and relays may also be designated by their _____ .

9. A solenoid designed to operate for 2 min or less is considered _____ -duty.

10. A solenoid that is designed to be left in the activated position for longer than 2 min is a _____ -duty solenoid.

11. _____ are a type of electronic switch with no moving contact points and are used in conjunction with electronic circuitry to detect the position of various moving components on an aircraft, such as flaps and landing gear.

12. A _____ exists when an accidental contact between conductors allows the current to return to the battery through a short, low-resistance path.

13. When the current flowing through a _____ exceeds the rated capacity, the metal strip inside melts and breaks the circuit.

14. A _____ serves a purpose similar to that of a fuse; however, it can usually be reset after a circuit fault is removed.

15. _____ circuit breakers cannot be reset until the temperature has returned to normal.

16. A _____ is a circuit element designed to insert resistance in the circuit.

17. The two important values associated with resistors are the value in _____ of resistance and the value in _____ , which represents the capacity of the resistor to dissipate power.

18. An _____ is usually of the wire-wound type, with a metal collar that can be moved along the resistance wire to vary the value of the resistance placed in the circuit.

19. A _____ is arranged so that it can be changed in value at any time by the operator of the electronic circuit.

20. A _____ is typically connected in a circuit merely to change the current flow and has a comparatively low resistance value (usually below 500 Ω).

21. A potentiometer normally is connected with _____ terminals.

22. _____ are simply two resistors placed in series with each other and in parallel with a voltage source.

23. A _____ consists of two conductors which are capable of holding an electric charge and which are separated by an insulating medium.

24. The air, or some other insulating material, between the plates of a capacitor is called the

_____ .

25. The ability of a capacitor to store an electric charge is called _____ (C).

26. The capacitance of a capacitor depends on three principal factors: the area of the _____ , the thickness of the dielectric, and the material of which the dielectric is composed.

27. There are two general types of capacitors: fixed and _____ .

28. When a relatively high capacitance is desired in a small physical size, an _____ capacitor is used.

29. The dielectric of an electrolytic capacitor is a liquid or paste known as an _____ .

30. _____ is the ability of a conductor to induce a voltage into itself when a change in current is applied to the inductor.

31. The effect of an inductance coil in a circuit depends on the _____ of wire in the coil, the current flowing in the coil, and the material used in the core.

32. A _____ is a device used to increase or decrease the voltage in an ac circuit.

33. A transformer consists of a _____ winding and a _____ winding on either a laminated soft-iron core or an annealed sheet-steel core.

34. A laminated core reduces the effect of _____ , which otherwise would cause considerable heat and a loss of power.

35. When the secondary of a transformer has more turns of wire than the primary and is used to increase voltage, the

transformer is called a _____ transformer.

36. When a transformer is used to reduce voltage, it is called a _____ transformer.

37. A _____ is a device that allows current to flow in one direction but will oppose, or stop, current flow in the opposite direction.

38. The term _____ refers to a device in which a solid material is used to control electric currents through the manipulation of electrons.

39. The principal semiconductor materials used for rectifiers are _____ and germanium.

40. The n-type material of a diode is known as the _____ and is the electron emitter, or negative connection.

41. The p-type material of a diode is the _____ and is the electron acceptor, or positive connection.

42. When two types of germanium or silicon are joined, a _____ is formed.

43. When a diode is connected in such a way that it conducts, it is _____ .

44. When a diode is connected in such a way as to prevent conduction, it is _____ .

45. When a single rectifier (diode) is placed in series with an ac circuit, the result is called _____ .

46. The _____ is a very small solid-state device that takes the place of, and will do the work of, a much larger electron tube.

47. A _____ is similar to an electric solenoid or relay; that is, it can act as a remote-control switch.

48. _____ is another function commonly performed by transistors and is defined as an increase in a signal's power.

49. Amplification in a transistor is called _____ .

50. A _____ is a semiconductor that is used for switching purposes.

51. A _____ diode will conduct electricity only under certain voltage conditions; hence it is ideal for use in voltage regulator circuits.

52. _____ are semiconductors that respond to light.

53. _____ are heat-sensitive devices used on some aircraft to monitor the temperature of certain electrical equipment.

54. Modern electronic equipment uses _____ , which provide a mounting surface and the electric current paths for the individual components of a system.

Chapter 6

MULTIPLE-CHOICE QUESTIONS

Circle the letter of the best answer.

1. The amount of electricity a capacitor can store is directly proportional to
   a. the distance between the plates and inversely proportional to the plate area.
   b. the plate area and is not affected by the distance between the plates.
   c. the plate area and inversely proportional to the distance between the plates.
   d. the distance between the plates and is not affected by the plate area.

2. A zener diode will only conduct current at a certain
   a. current level.
   b. temperature level.
   c. resistance level.
   d. voltage level.

3. A transformer with a step-up ratio of 5 to 1 has a primary voltage of 24 V and a secondary amperage of 0.20 A. What is the primary amperage (disregard losses)?
   a. 1 A
   b. 4.8 A
   c. 0.40 A
   d. Cannot be determined from the information given

4. Diodes are often used in electric power circuits primarily as
   a. current eliminators.
   b. circuit cutout switches.
   c. rectifiers.
   d. power transducer relays.

5. Which lead of a transistor will carry the majority of the current?
   a. Emitter
   b. Collector
   c. Anode
   d. Base

6. What happens to the current in a step-up transformer with a ratio of 1 to 4?
   a. The current is stepped down by a 1-to-4 ratio.
   b. The current is stepped up by a 1-to-4 ratio.
   c. The current does not change.
   d. The current is changed at half the voltage ratio.

7. Aircraft fuse capacity is rated in
   a. volts.
   b. ohms.
   c. amperes.
   d. microfarads.

8. When a rheostat is added to a light circuit to control the light intensity, it should be connected
   a. in parallel with the light.
   b. across the source of energy.
   c. in series with the light.
   d. in series-parallel with the light switch.

9. What kind of switch would you install in a single-wire circuit that required the switch to be manually held in the ON position?
   a. Single-pole, single-throw (SPST), two-position normally open (NO)
   b. Single-pole, single-throw (SPST), single-position
   c. Single-pole, double-throw (SPDT), two-position
   d. Single-pole, double-throw (SPDT), single-position normally open (NO)

10. A relay is
    a. a magnetically operated switch.
    b. a device that increases voltage.
    c. a device that converts electric energy to heat energy.
    d. any conductor that receives electric energy and passes it on with little or no resistance.

11. What is the voltage drop across the junction of a forward-biased silicon diode?
    a. 0.3 V
    b. 0.4 V
    c. 0.5 V
    d. 0.6 V

12. The purpose of a rectifier in an electrical system is to change
    a. the frequency of alternating current.
    b. the voltage of alternating current.
    c. the voltage and amperage of alternating current.
    d. alternating current to direct current.

13. When an electric switch is selected for installation in an aircraft circuit utilizing a dc motor,
    a. a switch designed for direct current should be chosen.
    b. the switch must be a single-pole, single-throw (SPST) type.
    c. a derating factor should be applied.
    d. only a switch with screw-type terminal connections should be used.

14. Circuit-protection devices are installed primarily to protect the
    a. relays.
    b. switches.
    c. units.
    d. wiring.

Chapter 6

Name _____

Date _____

APPLICATION QUESTIONS

1. Considering the switch derating factor, if a switch is needed to control a 24-V, 10-A motor, how many amps must the switch be rated for?

2. How many poles and throws are contained in the switches shown in the diagrams below?

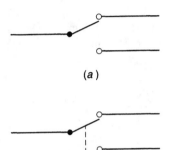

(a)

(b)

3. According to the wire protection chart below, (a) what is the maximum size of a circuit breaker that can be used for a 16-gage wire, and (b) what is the maximum size of a fuse for the same wire?

Wire AN gage: copper	Circuit breaker, A	Fuse, A
22	5	5
20	7.5	5
18	10	10
16	15	20
14	20	15
12	25(30)*	20
10	35(40)	30
8	50	50
6	80	70
4	100	70
2	125	100
1		150
0		150

*Figures in parentheses may be substituted where protectors of the indicated ratings are not available.

4. Is the variable resistor shown in the following diagram a rheostat or a potentiometer?

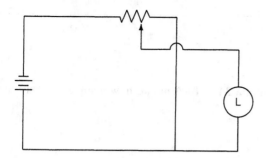

5. If a transformer has 100 turns in the primary and 300 turns in the secondary and uses a 115-V, 10-A input, what is the voltage and maximum current available at the output of the secondary? (Assume that the transformer is 100 percent efficient.)

6. Are the transformers shown below connected in series or parallel?

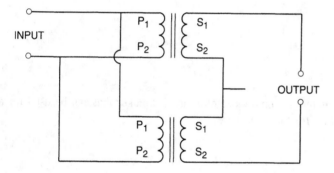

7. Assuming that current travels from negative to positive, label the direction of the current flow through the diodes and the load in the circuit below.

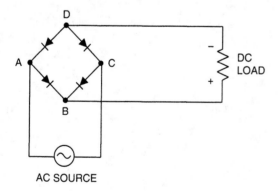

8. a. What type of transistor is shown by the diagram below?
   b. Identify the leads of the transistor in the diagram below.

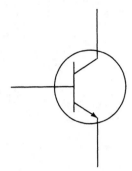

9. In order for the lamp in the following circuit to be at maximum brightness, in what position must the potentiometer be placed?

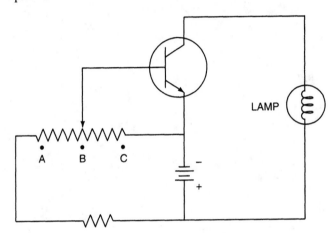

Chapter 7

Name _____

Date _____

STUDY QUESTIONS

1. A _____ signal is one that contains two distinct values: on and off, or 1 and 0.

2. An _____ signal is one that contains an infinite number of voltage values.

3. _____ are the fundamental components for all computers and utilize digital signals.

4. The _____ number system is composed of two components, 1 and 0.

5. One _____ is equal to one binary digit.

6. Bits handled as a group are referred to as a _____ .

7. A _____ is a grouping of bits that a computer uses as a standard information format.

8. The _____ decimal system uses a group of four bits to represent each digit of a decimal number.

9. The _____ notation system is a binary representation of an octal number.

10. The _____ number system uses base 16.

11. _____ gates are types of fundamental functions performed by computers and related equipment.

12. _____ tables are systematic means of displaying binary data.

13. The _____ gate is used to represent a situation where all inputs to the gate must be 1 (on) to produce a 1 (on) output.

14. The _____ gate is used to represent a situation where any input being on (1) will produce an on (1) output.

15. The _____ gate is used to reverse the condition of the input signal.

16. The INVERT gate is sometimes referred to as a _____ gate.

17. The _____ gate is an OR gate with an inverted output.

18. The _____ gate is an AND gate with an inverted output.

19. The _____ gate is designed to produce a 1 output whenever its input signals are dissimilar.

20. If _____ logic is used in a digital circuit, a binary 1 equals a high voltage level and a binary 0 equals a low voltage level.

21. The _____ logic concept defines binary 1 as the lower voltage value and binary 0 as the higher voltage value (more positive).

22. The truth table and the _____ graph are the two most common types of digital data displays.

23. An _____ circuit is simply an assembly of diodes and/or transistors combined into an extremely small package.

24. _____ imprints a circuit on a silicon wafer by focusing a pattern of light into a concentrated area.

25. Integrated circuits are divided into two classes called _____ .

26. Two common logic families are the TTL and _____ families.

27. A _____ logic, or TTL, circuit contains bipolar transistors as its primary elements.

28. A _____ is a metal-oxide semiconductor field-effect transistor (MOSFET) using both p and n channel inputs.

29. All ICs adhere to the _____ standard.

30. _____ mounted components are mounted with their electrical connections bent at a 90° angle, which allows them to sit flat on the PCB.

31. A _____ switch is a common switching device used in computers and logic circuits.

32. _____ are logic circuits that add binary digits.

33. _____ circuits are a combination of basic gates that subtract binary digits.

34. A _____ clock provides a stable frequency of binary 1s and 0s.

35. A _____ material is commonly used to control the pulse time of a logic circuit to produce a consistent binary 1 and 0 waveform.

36. _____ and flip-flop circuits are combinations of logic gates that perform basic memory functions for computers and peripherals.

37. _____ are typically very large scale ICs that contain thousands of gates arranged to perform specific functions.

38. _____ modules are miniature circuit boards that contain a multitude of microprocessors, ICs, and other electrical components assembled by machine into one unit.

39. All microprocessors are made up of at least three basic elements: the _____ , the arithmetic logic unit (ALU), and a memory.

40. The _____ processes and directs data according to requests made by the operator or another circuit in the system.

41. The _____ performs the various calculations of the binary numbers.

42. The _____ of a microprocessor may be one of two types, permanent or temporary.

43. The _____ memory provides information for the basic operations of the microprocessor.

44. The _____ memory is used as a "notepad" for the short-term storage of data needed during the manipulation of numbers.

45. The communication link between the components of a microprocessor is called the _____ .

46. A microprocessor uses a _____ , or clock circuit, which operates as a timing device to coordinate the activities of the system.

47. At power-up a microprocessor always starts at its _____ .

48. _____ are basically small programs that operate when called for by the CPU.

49. The _____ tells the individual elements when to send or receive messages on the data bus.

50. The _____ is needed to coordinate the data transmission activities.

51. _____ are typically devices that allow a computer to communicate with humans or other electronic devices.

52. Similar to the microprocessor, the _____ of any computer performs the actual addition and subtraction and other logic functions.

53. A computer's central processing unit can be divided into three essential subsystems: the central control unit, the memory, and the _____ .

54. A _____ system is used to coordinate the events performed by each section of a computer.

55. A _____ bus is typically used to provide the communication link between the central control unit and the various computer sections.

56. The memory of a CPU is often divided into two basic categories: _____ memory and nonvolatile memory.

57. The data in a _____ memory will not be destroyed when the computer is turned off.

58. The data in a _____ are lost whenever the computer loses electric power.

59. Semiconductor memory circuits are divided into two categories: random-access memory (RAM) and

_____ .

60. _____ memory is often considered a write-and-read memory.

61. A _____ memory is a nonvolatile semiconductor memory.

62. There is a special type of ROM known as _____ , which can be altered by the user, but only under special conditions.

63. Most digital communication data are transmitted in a _____ form, that is, only one binary digit at a time.

64. _____ transmission is a continuous-type transmission requiring two wires (or one wire and ground) for each signal to be sent.

65. The devices for sending and receiving serial data are called _____ and demultiplexers (DEMUXes).

66. The _____ bus is a two-wire connection between the multiplexer and the demultiplexer.

67. _____ is a corporation established by foreign and domestic airlines, aircraft manufacturers, and transport companies to aid in the standardization of aircraft systems.

68. An _____ data bus is a one-way communication link between a single transmitter and multiple receivers.

69. ARINC 629 permits up to 120 devices to share a _____ serial data bus, which can be up to 100 m long.

70. The _____ is used extensively in Collins general aviation electronic equipment.

71. The _____ is used for communications on much of the Sperry flight control equipment.

72. A _____ diagram is a simplified schematic of a complex digital circuit.

73. BITE systems are designed to provide fault _____ , fault _____ , and operational verification after defect repair.

74. Some newer aircraft, like the Boeing 747-400, incorporate a _____ , which monitors the individual BITE systems of various components and records the data in a central location.

75. The _____ is a common carry-on piece of test equipment used to troubleshoot digital systems.

76. A _____ measures one point in a circuit to determine its logic level (high or low).

77. A _____ is capable of measuring the logic levels of an entire integrated circuit.

78. _____ are emitted by virtually every radio broadcast tower in the world.

79. Many digital electronic devices are susceptible to damage from the discharge of static electricity and are known as

_____ parts.

Chapter 7

Name _____

Date _____

MULTIPLE-CHOICE QUESTIONS

Circle the letter of the best answer.

1. Which logic gate will give a 1 output whenever the two inputs are 1 and 0 or 0 and 1 ?
   a. AND
   b. OR
   c. Exclusive OR
   d. INVERT

2. When the higher voltage value is represented by a binary 1 and the lower voltage value is represented by a binary 0, the circuit is operating using what type of logic?
   a. Positive logic
   b. Negative logic
   c. Digital logic
   d. Binary logic

3. What is the decimal value of the binary number 110011?
   a. 55
   b. 51
   c. 15
   d. 22

4. Which of the following is *not* a common binary code system?
   a. Hexadecimal
   b. Binary-coded decimal
   c. Octal notation
   d. Decimal

5. Which ARINC data bus system is a two-way communication bus?
   a. ARINC 629
   b. ARINC 269
   c. ARINC 429
   d. ARINC 129

6. Which logic symbol would be used to represent two switches in series used to turn on a light?
   a. The AND gate
   b. The OR gate
   c. The NAND gate
   d. The NOR gate

7. A circuit that operates using two distinct signals is called a(n)
   a. digital circuit.
   b. decimal circuit.
   c. analog circuit.
   d. binary circuit.

8. What is the decimal value of 2^3?
   a. 4
   b. 6
   c. 16
   d. 8

9. Circuits that operate using transistor-transistor logic (TTL) use what voltage to represent binary 1?
   a. −5 V
   b. 0 V
   c. +5 V
   d. +18 V

10. The development of what type of component has made it possible to effectively use both sides of a printed circuit board?
    a. Integrated circuit
    b. Microprocessor
    c. DIP standard component
    d. Surface mounted component

11. Binary digits are often referred to as which of the following terms?
    a. Bits
    b. Bytes
    c. Words
    d. Sentences

12. What type of memory is lost when the power to the computer is turned off?
    a. Volatile memory
    b. Transistor memory
    c. Read-only memory
    d. Random-access memory

13. Typically during start-up, a microprocessor begins operations with which of the following?
    a. Subroutine
    b. Initializing routine
    c. Synchronizing routine
    d. Address routine

14. Which section of a computer performs the actual addition and subtraction functions of a program?
    a. Central control unit
    b. Peripherals
    c. Data bus
    d. Central processing unit

Chapter 7

APPLICATION QUESTIONS

1. What is the output of the following AND gate?

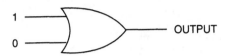

1 —
0 —
OUTPUT

2. Determine the truth table and name the logic gate for the following waveform graph.

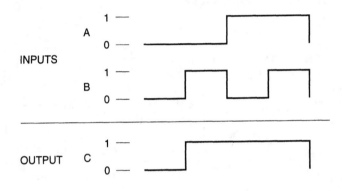

INPUTS

A

1 —
0 —

B

1 —
0 —

OUTPUT   C

1 —
0 —

3. Determine the output for the following digital circuit.

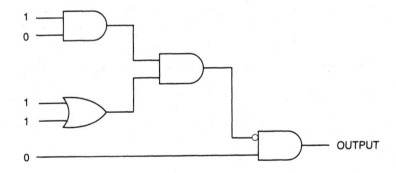

1 —
0 —

1 —
1 —

0 —

OUTPUT

4. What is the output for the exclusive OR gate below?

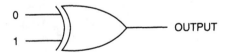

0 —
1 —
OUTPUT

5. The following circuit represents which logic gate?

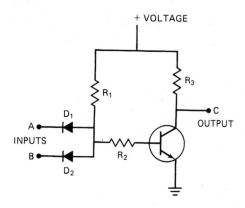

6. Would the parity bit be a binary 0 or 1 for the following ARINC 429 message below?

BINARY WORD

32	31 30 29	28 27 26 25 24 23 22 21 20 19 18 17 16 15 14 13 12 11	10 9	8 7 6 5 4 3 2 1
P	SSM	←——————————— DATA ———————————→	SDI	←——— LABEL ———→
	1 1 1	1 0 1 0 1 1 0	0 1	0 1 1 0 0 1 1 0

7. What is the value of the computed airspeed for the ARINC 429 message below?

BINARY WORD

32	31 30 29	28 27 26 25 24 23 22 21 20 19 18 17 16 15 14 13 12 11	10 9	8 7 6 5 4 3 2 1
P	SSM	←——————————— DATA ———————————→	SDI	←——— LABEL ———→
0	1 1 0	0 1 0 0 1 0 0 0 1 1	0 0	0 1 1 0 0 0 0 1

Chapter 8

Name _____

Date _____

STUDY QUESTIONS

1. The common electric measuring instruments are the ammeter, voltmeter, ohmmeter, and

   _____ .

2. A _____ is a device that reacts to minute electromagnetic influences caused within itself by the flow of a small amount of current.

3. The most common types of electric measuring instruments employ a moving coil and a permanent magnet known as

   the _____ or Weston movement.

4. A movement similar to the d'Arsonval movement, but suitable for ac measurements, employs an electromagnet in

   place of the permanent magnet and is called a _____ movement.

5. An _____ mechanism employs an iron vane through which electromagnetic forces act to move the indicating needle.

6. In this instrument movement, the moving coil is suspended on a taut platinum-iridium band held by spring tension in

   the instrument frame and is called a _____ .

7. _____ is determined by the amount of current required to produce a full-scale deflection of the indicating needle.

8. When a resistor is connected in parallel with the terminals of a meter, it is called a _____ .

9. A shunt resistor, also called an _____ , can be defined as a particular type of resistor designed to be connected in parallel with a meter to extend the current range beyond some particular value for which the instrument is already competent.

10. In general, the word _____ means connected in parallel.

11. A _____ of the moving-coil type actually measures the current flow through the instrument; but since the current flow is proportional to the voltage, the instrument dial may be marked in volts.

12. The range of a voltmeter can be increased by the use of additional series resistors called

    _____ .

13. The _____ is an instrument for measuring resistance.

14. Testing _____ is the process whereby the meter is used to determine if the circuit has a complete (continuous) current path.

15. The _____ meter was one of the first movements used for high-frequency (HF) ac measurements that was not adversely affected by the frequency of the current.

16. One of the most common instruments for use with relatively low-frequency alternating currents is called a

    _____ instrument.

17. Some meters contain a test probe called an _____ or a current transformer that wraps around one wire of the circuit to be tested.

18. _____ counters are instruments used to "count" the electrical pulses of a given voltage.

19. The functions of a voltmeter, an ohmmeter, and an ammeter (or milliammeter) are usually combined in an instrument

    called a _____ or volt-ohm-milliammeter (VOM).

20. A _____ probe is a type of inductive pickup that can be used to measure either ac or dc current.

21. The _____ is a sophisticated voltmeter with a two-dimensional graph display that can be used to measure the voltage (amplitude) and frequency (time) of an electric signal.

22. Nonelectrical phenomena such as sound or temperature can be measured with specialized probes called

_____ .

Chapter 8

Name _____

Date _____

MULTIPLE-CHOICE QUESTIONS

Circle the letter of the best answer.

1. How should a voltmeter be connected?
   a. In series with the source
   b. In parallel with the load
   c. In series with the load
   d. In series-parallel with the source

2. Which meter would be used to test for continuity of a wire?
   a. Voltmeter
   b. Ammeter
   c. Wattmeter
   d. Ohmmeter

3. The oscilloscope is a sophisticated voltmeter with a two-dimensional graph display that can be used to measure which of the following of an electric signal?
   a. Voltage and frequency
   b. Voltage and resistance
   c. Resistance and current
   d. Voltage and power

4. The inductive pickup used on some electric measuring instruments works on what principle?
   a. Thermoelectric effect
   b. Expansion and contraction of dissimilar metals
   c. Electromagnetic induction
   d. Magnetic attraction and repulsion of ferrous metals

5. What type of instrument is used for measuring very high-values of resistance?
   a. Megaohmmeter
   b. Shunt-type ohmmeter
   c. Thermocouple
   d. Multimeter

6. What characteristic of a digital meter will determine how small of a measurement the meter can make?
   a. The sensitivity
   b. The current rating
   c. The resolution
   d. The voltage rating

7. The sensitivity of a meter is determined by the amount of current required to produce which of the following?
   a. A 1-V deflection of the indicating needle
   b. A full-scale deflection of the indicating needle
   c. A 1-Ω deflection of the indicating needle
   d. A midscale deflection of the indicating needle

8. Shunts must be used on a typical multimeter when measuring
   a. high current.
   b. low current.
   c. high voltage.
   d. low voltage.

Chapter 8

APPLICATION QUESTIONS

1. What characteristic of the following circuit will a multimeter provide?

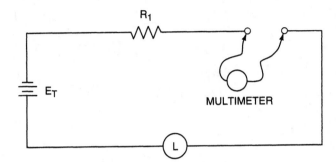

2. What characteristic of the following circuit will a multimeter provide?

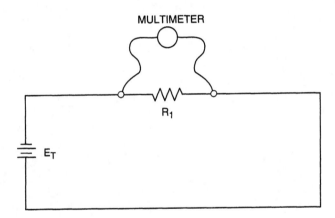

3. Describe why this is not an accurate way to measure the continuity of the lamp in the following circuit.

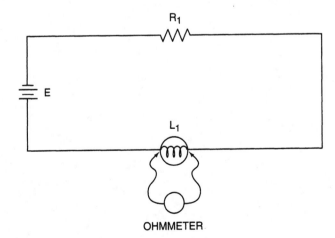

Chapter 9

Name _____

Date _____

STUDY QUESTIONS

1. An _____ motor is a device that changes electric power to mechanical energy.

2. There are series-wound, shunt-wound, and _____ motors, named according to the relationship between the field coil connections and the armature winding.

3. Electric motors utilize the principles of magnetism and _____ induction.

4. The direction in which a current-carrying conductor in a magnetic field tends to move may be determined by the use of the _____ .

5. Because of the ability of a shunt motor to maintain an almost constant speed under a variety of loads, it is often called a _____ motor.

6. On light aircraft, motors used for the operation of landing gear, flaps, cowl flaps, and certain other types of apparatus must be designed to operate in either direction and are therefore called _____ motors.

7. Motors subject to sudden heavy loads are usually equipped with an overload release clutch, or _____ , and its function is to disconnect the motor from the driven mechanism when the load is great enough to cause damage.

8. Because of the limited distance of travel permitted in the driven mechanism, reversible actuating motors are usually limited in their amount of rotation in each direction by _____ switches.

9. Some actuating motors are provided with a thermal circuit breaker, or _____ protector, to protect the motor from overload and excessive heat.

10. There are three principal types of ac motors: the universal motor, the induction motor, and the _____ motor.

11. A _____ motor is identical with a dc motor and can be operated on either alternating or direct current.

12. The percentage of difference in the speeds of the stator and rotor fields is called the _____ .

13. The _____ point is when the load on an induction motor becomes so great that the torque of the rotor cannot carry it, and so the motor will stop.

14. Motors that employ capacitors for starting or for continuous operation are often called _____ motors.

15. A _____ motor utilizes the repulsion of like poles to produce the torque for operation.

16. _____ motors, as the name implies, rotate at a speed that is synchronized with the applied alternating current.

17. The power used to overcome the friction of bearings is called the _____ loss.

18. The loss due to wind friction is sometimes called _____ loss and is comparatively high when a motor is equipped with a fan to provide cooling by forced ventilation.

19. The power used to overcome the resistance of the windings is called resistance, or _____ , loss.

20. The current induced in the armature core and the field poles is called _____ and is responsible for considerable loss in the form of heat.

21. _____ occur when a material is magnetized first in one direction and then in the other in rapid succession.

22. The _____ motor consists essentially of a three-phase Y-wound stator and a conventional squirrel-cage rotor.

Chapter 9

Name _____

Date _____

MULTIPLE-CHOICE QUESTIONS

Circle the letter of the best answer.

1. Which of the following is true concerning a thermal protector for a motor?
   a. The thermal protector replaces the circuit breaker for the motor.
   b. The thermal protector will open the motor's circuit during an overload condition.
   c. A thermal protector is used only on a dc motor.
   d. A thermal protector is used only on an ac motor.

2. Which of the following is a true statement concerning split-phase motors?
   a. They are dc motors.
   b. They are commonly used for starter motors.
   c. They are ac motors.
   d. They are reverisble motors.

3. Some electric motors have two sets of field windings wound in opposite directions so that the
   a. speed of the motor can be more closely controlled.
   b. power output of the motor can be more closely controlled.
   c. motor can be operated at any speed within its rated range without a change in power output.
   d. motor can be operated in either direction.

4. What type of dc motor is commonly referred to as a constant-speed motor?
   a. Series-wound motor
   b. Synchronous motor
   c. Shunt-wound motor
   d. Universal motor

5. One purpose of a growler test is to determine the presence of
   a. an out-of-round commutator.
   b. a broken field lead.
   c. a shorted armature.
   d. a short from F+ to A−.

6. What are the general types of ac motors used in aircraft systems?
   a. Induction and synchronous
   b. Shaded pole and universal
   c. AC series and capacitor start
   d. Rheostat series and condenser start

7. The speed of a synchronous ac motor is determined by what characteristic of the motor circuit?
   a. The voltage of the circuit
   b. The current flow of the circuit
   c. The frequency of the applied voltage
   d. The resistance of the motor circuit

8. What type of aircraft utilizes three-phase ac motors?
   a. Light single-engine aircraft
   b. Light twin-engine aircraft
   c. Large transport-category aircraft
   d. Turboprop commuter aircraft

9. How can the direction of rotation of a dc electric motor be changed?
   a. Interchange the wires that connect the motor to the external power source.
   b. Reverse the electrical connections to either the field or armature windings.
   c. Rotate the brush assembly 90°.
   d. Remove the starting winding.

10. A certain dc series motor mounted within an aircraft draws more amperes during start than when it is running under its rated load. The most logical conclusion that may be drawn is that
    a. the starting winding is shorted.
    b. the brushes are floating at operating rpm because of weak brush springs.
    c. the condition is normal for this type of motor.
    d. hysteresis losses have become excessive through armature bushing (or bearing) wear.

11. What type of electric motor is generally used with a direct-cranking engine starter?
    a. DC shunt-wound motor
    b. DC series-wound motor
    c. DC compound-wound motor
    d. Synchronous motor

12. Arcing at the brushes and burning of the commutator of a motor may be caused by
    a. weak brush springs.
    b. excessive brush spring tension.
    c. a smooth commutator.
    d. low mica.

13. The direction in which a wire carrying current will move when acted on by a magnetic field is determined by which of the following?
    a. The electron theory
    b. The right-hand motor rule
    c. The left-hand motor rule
    d. The magnetic motor rule

14. What is the principal advantage of the series-wound dc motor?
    a. High starting torque
    b. Suitable for constant-speed use
    c. Low starting torque
    d. Speed slightly higher when unloaded

15. What is the effect of a counter emf in a motor?
    a. It strengthens the applied voltage.
    b. It opposes the applied voltage.
    c. It strengthens the applied current.
    d. It increases the motor's speed of rotation.

16. What is the purpose of a split field in a dc motor?
    a. To reverse the motor's rotation
    b. To increase the starting torque of the motor
    c. To decrease the counter emf of the motor
    d. To increase the motor's speed of rotation

Chapter 9

APPLICATION QUESTIONS

1. Draw the schematic of a reversible dc motor that employs two field windings. Identify the armature, the clockwise and counterclockwise field windings, the power source, and the control switch.

2. Draw the schematic of a simple series-wound motor. Label the armature and field windings.

3. Identify the components on the diagram of the starter motor below.

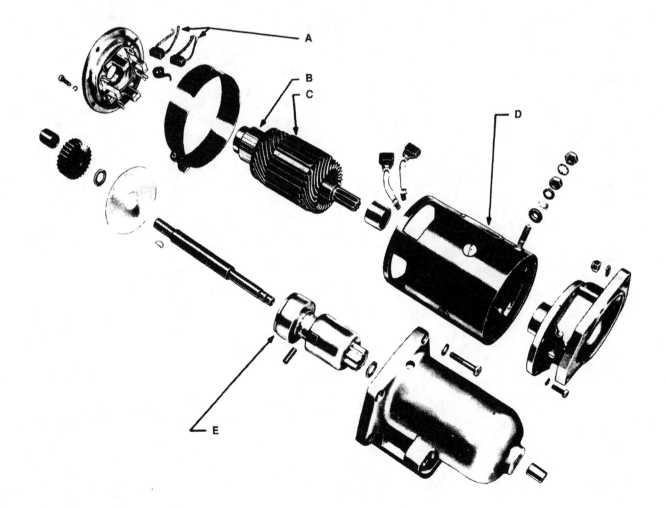

Chapter 10

STUDY QUESTIONS

1. An electric generator can be defined as a machine that changes mechanical energy into

   _____ energy.

2. Electricity is produced in a generator by _____ induction.

3. A simple way to determine the direction of current flow is to use the _____ rule for generators.

4. The _____ field in a generator is produced by a permanent magnet or by electromagnet field coils.

5. The rotating loop or coil in a generator is called the _____ , or rotor, and receives the induced current.

6. The _____ in a generator are in contact with the rotating armature and carry the current to the aircraft's electrical bus.

7. The poles of a magnet are called _____ .

8. In most generators, the field poles are wound with coils of wire called _____ .

9. The voltage induced in a conductor moving across a magnetic field depends on two principal factors: the strength of

   the field and the _____ with which the conductor moves across the lines of force.

10. A _____ is a switching device that reverses the external connections to the armature at the same time that the current reverses in the armature.

11. The system of changing the alternating current of the armature to direct current in the external circuit is called

    _____ .

12. Materials such as soft iron give up most of their magnetism very quickly when removed from the magnetizing influ-

    ence, but they do retain a small amount, which is known as _____ magnetism.

13. DC generators are classified as shunt-wound, series-wound, or _____ , according to the manner of connecting the field coils with respect to the armature.

14. The magnetic field in the armature is at right angles to the generator field shown and is called

    _____ of the armature.

15. The neutral plane is the position where the armature windings are moving parallel to the magnetic flux lines and is

    known as _____ , which is proportional to the current flowing in the armature coils.

16. The use of _____ is the most satisfactory method for maintaining a constant neutral plane in a generator.

17. In many generators, a _____ is used to help overcome armature reaction.

18. The heavy iron or steel housing that supports the field poles is called the field frame, field ring, or

    _____ .

19. The generator _____ support the armature bearings and are mounted at each end of the field frame.

20. _____ are a combination of a generator and starter housed in one unit.

21. Some starter-generators employ a drive shaft _____ , which is used to protect the engine's gear box in the event the generator mechanically fails and cannot rotate.

22. In a generator, the voltage produced depends on three factors: (*a*) the _____ at which the armature rotates, (*b*) the number of _____ in series in the armature, and (*c*) the _____ of the magnetic field.

23. In every system in which a generator is used to charge batteries as well as to supply operating power, a _____ relay must be provided for disconnecting the generator from the battery when the generator voltage is lower than the battery voltage.

24. In some generator systems a _____ device is installed that will reduce the generator voltage whenever the maximum safe load is exceeded.

25. A _____ consists of a voltage regulator, a current limiter, and a reverse-current cutout relay mounted as a single unit.

26. A starter-generator is regulated by the _____ .

27. The process of balancing generators is often referred to as _____ the generators.

28. The amount of _____ visible indicates the service life remaining on that particular brush.

29. _____ brushes contain a lubricating additive that improves brush conductivity and wear characteristics.

Chapter 10

MULTIPLE-CHOICE QUESTIONS

Circle the letter of the best answer.

1. To what depth is the mica insulation between the commutator bars of a dc generator undercut?
   a. One-half the width of the mica
   b. Approximately 0.25 in.
   c. Approximately 0.02 in.
   d. Never undercut

2. A voltage regulator controls generator output by
   a. introducing a resistance in generator-to-battery lead in the event of overload.
   b. shorting out field coil in the event of overload.
   c. varying current flow to the generator field coil.
   d. motorizing generator to oppose its action.

3. In installations where the ammeter is in the generator or alternator lead and the regulator system does not limit the maximum current that the generator or alternator can deliver, the ammeter can be redlined at
   a. 50.
   b. 60.
   c. 75.
   d. 100.

4. What is a method used for restoring generator field residual magnetism?
   a. Flash the field(s).
   b. Demagnetize the commutator.
   c. Reseat the brushes.
   d. Energize the armature.

5. A voltage regulator controls generator voltage by changing the
   a. resistance in the generator output circuit.
   b. residual magnetism of the generator.
   c. current in the generator output circuit.
   d. resistance of the generator field circuit.

6. Starter-generators are typically found on which of the following types of aircraft?
   a. Piston-engine aircraft
   b. Large transport-category aircraft
   c. Turboprop aircraft
   d. Experimental aircraft

7. The poles of a generator are laminated to
   a. reduce hysteresis losses.
   b. reduce flux losses.
   c. increase flux concentration.
   d. reduce eddy current losses.

8. Residual voltage is a result of
   a. magnetism in the field windings.
   b. current flow in the field coils.
   c. magnetism in the field core.
   d. magnetism in the armature.

9. What device is used to convert alternating current, which has been induced into the loops of the rotating armature of a dc generator, into direct current?
   a. An alternator
   b. A rectifier
   c. A commutator
   d. An inverter

10. If the points in a vibrator-type voltage regulator stick in the closed position while the generator is operating, what will be the probable result?
    a. Generator output voltage will decrease.
    b. Generator output voltage will not be affected.
    c. Generator output voltage will increase.
    d. The reverse-current cutout relay will remove the generator from the line.

11. Assuming that all systems are operating normally, as the aircraft's electrical load is increased, the generator output voltage will
    a. decrease and the amperage output will increase.
    b. increase and the amperage output will increase.
    c. remain constant and the amperage output will increase.
    d. remain constant and the amperage output will decrease.

12. What is the purpose of a reverse-current cutout relay?
    a. It eliminates the possibility of reversed polarity of the generator output current.
    b. It prevents overloading of the generator.
    c. It prevents fluctuations of generator voltage.
    d. It opens the main generator circuit whenever the generator voltage drops below the battery voltage.

13. If a generator is equipped with a vibrator-type voltage regulator, the actual time the voltage regulator points remain open
    a. depends on the load carried by the generator.
    b. is controlled by the current limiter point clearance.
    c. is controlled by the reverse-current cutout relay point clearance.
    d. is increased when the external load is greater than the generator output.

14. The only practical method of maintaining a constant voltage output from an aircraft generator under varying conditions of speed and load is to vary the
    a. strength of the magnetic field.
    b. number of conductors in the armature.
    c. speed at which the armature rotates.
    d. brush pressure on the commutator segments.

15. What types of brushes can be replaced on a starter-generator without seating?
    a. Carbon brushes
    b. Instant seating brushes
    c. Instant filming brushes
    d. Copper brushes

Chapter 10

APPLICATION QUESTIONS

1. Draw a schematic diagram of a simple shunt-wound generator, and label the armature and field windings.

2. Identify components *a, b,* and *c* of the three-unit generator regulator in the diagram below.

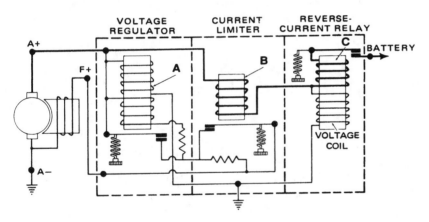

3. Identify components *a–l* of the typical generator shown below.

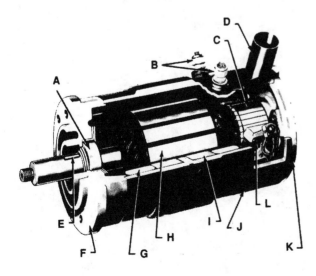

4. For the circuit below, what would the ammeter indicate for the following set of conditions?
   a. Battery near full charge, 20 A of electrical equipment operating, and all systems operating normally.
   b. Battery near full charge, 20 A of electrical equipment operating, and the alternator system inoperative.

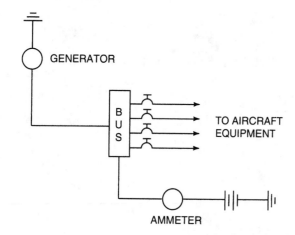

Chapter 11

Name _____

Date _____

STUDY QUESTIONS

1. There are two major types of alternators currently used on aircraft, the dc alternator and the

   _____ alternator.

2. _____ induction occurs when a conductor is cut by magnetic lines of force and a voltage is induced in the conductor, with the direction of the induced voltage depending on the direction of the magnetic flux and the direction of movement across the flux.

3. Almost all alternators for aircraft power systems are constructed with a _____ and a stationary armature.

4. Since a steady voltage must be provided for an aircraft's electrical system, the field strength of the alternator must be

   controlled by a _____ .

5. In an alternator the field rotates and is called the _____ .

6. To use alternator output current in a light-aircraft power system, it must first be converted into direct current by

   means of a _____ .

7. The rotor receives current through a pair of brushes, which will contact the field coil through

   _____ .

8. A _____ voltage regulator contains a field relay that supplies current to the transistor, and the transistor controls the current to the field.

9. An _____ not only regulates alternator output voltage but also turns off the charging system if an overvoltage condition exists.

10. For emergency situations ac generators driven by auxiliary power units (APUs) or _____ are often used.

11. The number of cycles of alternating current per second is called the _____ .

12. _____ alternators were developed for the purpose of eliminating some of the problems of alternators that employ slip rings and brushes to carry exciter current to the rotating field.

13. In order to provide constant-speed generator operation in modern ac electrical systems, it is common practice to use a

    _____ .

14. Most CSDs are equipped with a _____ adapter, which allows the technician to remove and replace a generator and CSD assembly in a matter of minutes.

15. The _____ is a state-of-the-art means of producing ac electric power.

16. The _____ has functions such as voltage regulation, current limiting, protection for out-of-tolerance voltage and frequency conditions, and crew alerting.

17. In the case of a generator system failure, the GCU senses partial loss of electric power and automatically sends the

    appropriate signal to the _____ .

18. An _____ is a device for converting direct current into alternating current at the frequency and voltage required for particular purposes.

19. The internal circuitry of a _____ inverter contains standard electric and electronic components such as crystal diodes, transistors, capacitors, and transformers.

20. _____ are typically referred to as VSCF systems.

Chapter 11

Name _____

Date _____

MULTIPLE-CHOICE QUESTIONS

Circle the letter of the best answer.

1. The voltage output of an alternator may be regulated by controlling the
   a. speed of the alternator.
   b. current of the field circuit.
   c. resistance in the rotor windings.
   d. exciter frequency.

2. A CSD is used to drive a typical ac alternator in order to maintain which of the following?
   a. A constant voltage
   b. A constant current
   c. A constant frequency
   d. A constant wattage

3. An integrated drive generator (IDG) combines which of the following units into one housing?
   a. The generator and the voltage regulator
   b. The generator and the constant-speed drive
   c. The GCU and the constant-speed drive
   d. The GCU and the alternator

4. What is typically used to cool an IDG?
   a. Water
   b. Oil
   c. Air
   d. Hydraulic fluid

5. A VSCF alternator system uses which of the following to maintain a constant ac frequency?
   a. Solid-state electronic circuits
   b. A constant-speed drive
   c. A generator control unit
   d. A frequency control unit

6. What is the frequency of an alternator dependent on?
   a. Voltage
   b. rpm
   c. Current
   d. Wattage rating

7. What type of rectifier is employed on a dc alternator?
   a. Three-phase, half-wave
   b. Three-phase, full-wave
   c. Single-phase, half-wave
   d. Single-phase, full-wave

8. How many diodes are used in the rectifier for a dc alternator?
   a. 3
   b. 6
   c. 1
   d. 4

9. How are the rotor windings of an aircraft alternator usually excited?
   a. By a constant ac voltage from the battery
   b. With alternating current from a permanent condenser
   c. By a constant ac voltage
   d. By a variable direct current

10. What is the frequency of most aircraft alternating currents?
    a. 115 Hz
    b. 120 Hz
    c. 220 Hz
    d. 400 Hz

11. Most light-aircraft dc alternators contain which of the following?
    a. A stationary field
    b. A permanent-magnet field
    c. A rotating field
    d. A three-phase field

12. Which of the following is not a component used in a dc alternator?
    a. Commutator
    b. Rectifier
    c. Brush
    d. Armature

13. Which instrument would be used to test a field winding of a dc alternator after disassembly?
    a. Voltmeter
    b. Ammeter
    c. Ohmmeter
    d. Growler

14. How does a voltage regulator control the output of a dc alternator?
    a. By varying the resistance of the armature circuit
    b. By varying the resistance of the rectifier circuit
    c. By varying the resistance of the stator circuit
    d. By varying the resistance of the field circuit

15. What types of aircraft are most likely to employ an ac alternator?
    a. Transport-category aircraft
    b. Corporate aircraft
    c. Light single-engine aircraft
    d. Light twin-engine aircraft

16. What is the output voltage across two phases of a typical permanent-magnet generator?
    a. 208 V
    b. 115 V
    c. 230 V
    d. 400 V

17. The part of a dc alternator power system that prevents the reverse flow of current from the battery to the alternator is the
    a. reverse-current cutout relay.
    b. voltage regulator.
    c. differential reverse-current relay.
    d. rectifier.

18. What device is used to change direct current to alternating current?
    a. An ac-dc alternator
    b. A dc-ac alternator
    c. An inverter
    d. A transformer

Chapter 11

APPLICATION QUESTION

1. Identify components *a–h* of the alternator shown below.

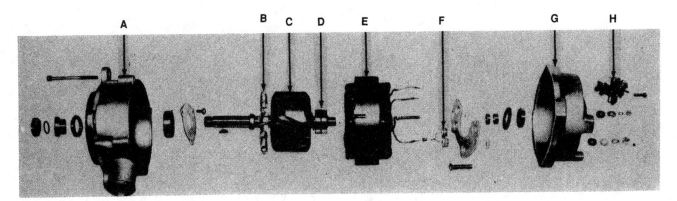

Chapter 12

Name _____

Date _____

STUDY QUESTIONS

1. A simple power distribution system consists of a basic copper conductor called a _____ , or bus.

2. The metal airframe (negative side of the voltage) is often referred to as the _____ ; hence this type of distribution system is often called a _____ ground system.

3. In all negative ground aircraft, the positive voltage is distributed to the electric equipment through insulated wires, and the negative is connected through the _____ .

4. Since only one wire (and the ground) is needed to operate electric equipment in negative ground aircraft, this type of wiring is known as a _____ -wire system.

5. The general requirements for power distribution systems on normal utility and acrobatic aircraft are set forth by FAR _____ .

6. FAR _____ establishes the power distribution requirements for transport-category aircraft.

7. Further requirements for electrical systems in transport-category aircraft specify that the generating capacity for the system and the number and kinds of power sources must be determined by a _____ .

8. It must be shown by analysis, tests, or both that an aircraft can be operated safely in VFR (visual flight rules) conditions for a period of not less than _____ min with the normal electric power sources, excluding the battery, inoperative.

9. A Boeing 727 with a fully charged battery can operate all essential electrical systems for approximately _____ min without supplemental power from any generator.

10. A circuit-protective device must be the _____ type, which cannot be overridden manually.

11. When fuses are used in an aircraft electrical system, spare fuses must be provided for use in flight in a quantity equal to at least _____ of the number of fuses of each rating required for complete circuit protection.

12. Each circuit for _____ loads must have individual circuit protection; however, individual protection for each circuit in an essential load system is not required.

13. A _____ switch must be provided that will make it possible to disconnect all power sources from the distribution system.

14. Examples of _____ loads are navigation lights, the rotating beacon, the radio receiver, radio navigation equipment, electric instruments, electric fuel pumps, electric vacuum pumps, the air-conditioning system, and all other units or systems that can be operated continuously during flight.

15. _____ loads are those which are operated for 2 min or less and are then turned off.

16. It is recommended that the _____ continuous load be not more than 80 percent of the generator capacity on aircraft where special placards or monitoring devices are not installed.

17. Aircraft that employ an _____ to monitor the charging system status can operate continuous electrical loads up to 100 percent of the generator capacity.

18. An ammeter should be _____ so that the pilot can determine easily when an overload exists.

19. Prior to installing any electric equipment in an aircraft, the technician must perform an _____ .

20. Whenever a switch is opened or closed within a relay or solenoid coil circuit, a _____ , or transient voltage, is produced.

21. The fuselage and wing assemblies of the Beechcraft Starship employ a _____ because the composite materials have too high of a resistance to easily carry current.

22. Two methods are used to connect electric equipment to the ground plane: _____ electrical bonding and _____ electrical bonding.

23. The indirect method uses flexible metal straps called _____ to connect the ground plane to the electric component.

24. Two basic configurations are used to distribute electric power in transport-category aircraft: the _____ system and the _____ system.

25. In a _____ electric power distribution system, all ac generators are connected to one distribution bus.

26. A tie bus is often referred to as a _____ bus; its purpose is to connect the output of all operating generators.

27. The _____ buses are used to distribute the generator current to the various electrical loads.

28. All aircraft electrical systems are designed with a bus _____ , which allows the most critical components to be the least likely to fail.

29. In the event of a system overload, the control unit must reduce the electrical load to an acceptable level, a process known as load _____ .

30. Load _____ are electric circuits that sense real system current and provide control signals for the generator's constant-speed drive rpm governor.

31. A _____ power transfer means that the automated system can change the ac power source without a momentary interruption of electric power.

Chapter 12

Name _____

Date _____

Circle the letter of the best answer.

1. What instrument is typically used to indicate to appropriate flight crew members the electrical quantities in the system essential for safe operation of the aircraft?
   a. A voltmeter
   b. A wattmeter
   c. An ohmmeter
   d. An ammeter

2. A diode installed in parallel with the coil of a relay is used to
   a. eliminate the relay contact points.
   b. reduce point bounce.
   c. eliminate voltage spikes.
   d. reduce arcing at the contact points.

3. How long can a typical Boeing 727 with a fully charged battery operate all essential electrical systems without supplemental power from any generator?
   a. 30 min
   b. 60 min
   c. 5 min
   d. 20 min

4. Which of the following states the purpose of an electrical-load analysis?
   a. To determine the output of the aircraft generators
   b. To determine that the essential electrical loads will not discharge the aircraft's battery
   c. To determine that the aircraft's electric power system will not be overloaded
   d. To determine the intermittent loads of the aircraft

5. Which units are used to sense the current flow through the main power leads of a transport-category aircraft?
   a. Relays
   b. Contactors
   c. Load controllers
   d. Current transformers

6. Which of the following is true concerning a single-wire electrical system?
   a. The aircraft's metal structure is used to distribute the negative voltage signal.
   b. The battery is only connected at the positive terminal.
   c. One wire is used to connect all electric components to the positive bus.
   d. The positive bus consists of one wire.

7. Which FAR specifies the general requirements for the electric power distribution system found on transport-category aircraft?
   a. FAR Part 23
   b. FAR Part 65
   c. FAR Part 43
   d. FAR Part 25

8. What does the Beechcraft Starship use for a ground plane?
   a. A steel wire bonded into the composite structure of the airframe
   b. An aluminum mesh bonded to the composite material
   c. A copper mesh bonded to the composite material
   d. An aluminum wire routed through the composite material

9. On most large aircraft, which units are used to change the ac voltage produced by the generators to 28-V dc power?
   a. Rectifier units
   b. DC couplers
   c. R-T units
   d. T-R units

10. Which is a true statement concerning the split bus power distribution system?
    a. The aircraft generators are never connected to the same distribution bus.
    b. The aircraft generators are connected to the same bus only in emergency situations.
    c. There is no need for an emergency bus, since the system uses two independent buses.
    d. The aircraft generators typically operate connected to the same bus.

11. When is the hot battery bus on the Boeing 727 connected to the battery?
    a. Only during flight
    b. Always
    c. Only during emergency operations
    d. Never

12. On most light single-engine aircraft, the master switch contains two independent poles and throws. These two independent poles and throws are used to control which of the following?
    a. The battery master solenoid and the alternator voltage regulator
    b. The battery master solenoid and the radio equipment master solenoid
    c. The avionics master solenoid and the alternator voltage regulator
    d. The battery master solenoid and the starter solenoid

Name _____

Date _____

Using the power distribution system schematic below for reference, answer questions 1–3 on page 80.

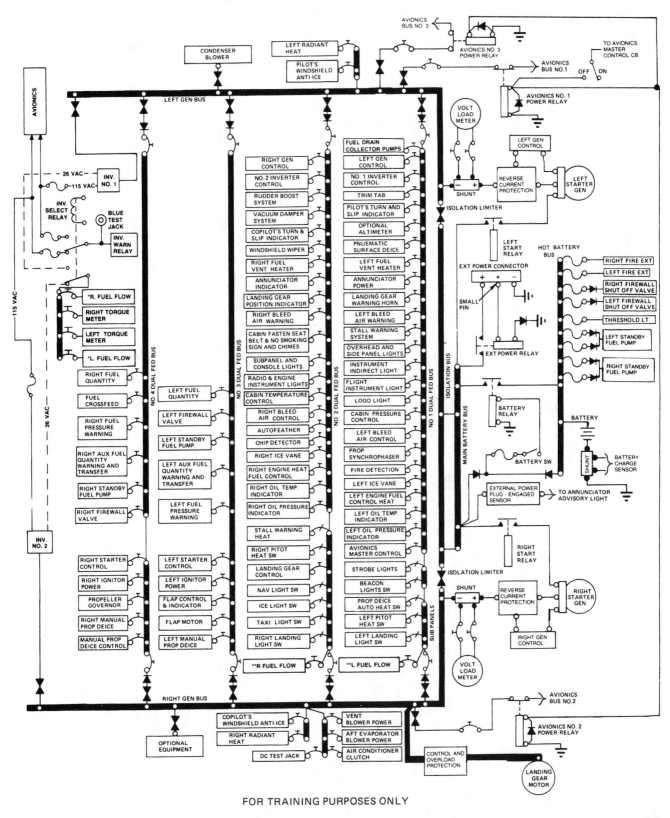

FOR TRAINING PURPOSES ONLY

1. Can current travel from the left generator bus to the right generator bus through the No. 3 dual feed bus?

2. What is the purpose of the two isolation limiters connected to the isolation bus?

3. Which bus is used to power the avionics master control?

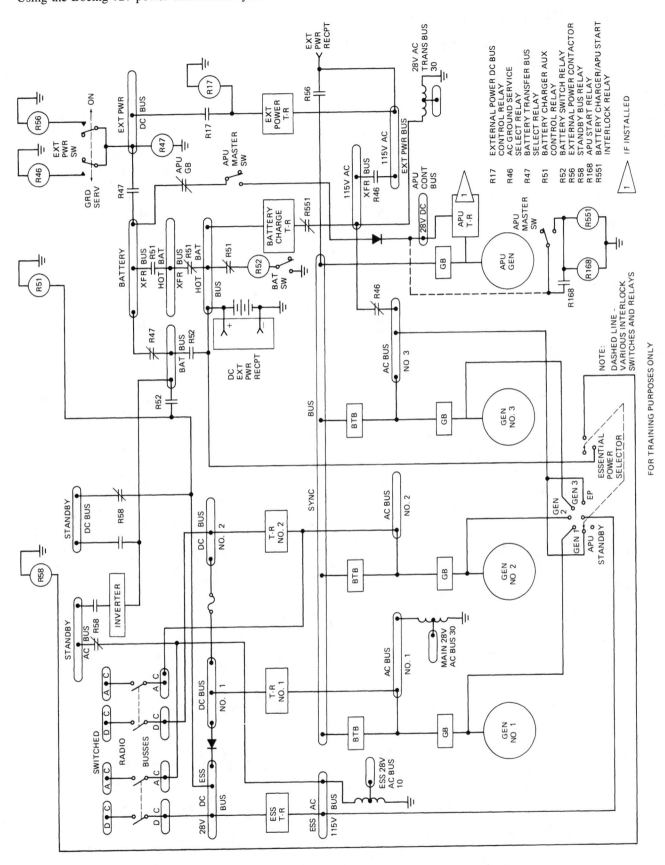

4. What do the dashed lines on the schematic represent?

5. Is this a split bus or parallel distribution system?

6. Which contactors must be closed to connect generator no. 2 to the sync bus?

Chapter 13

Name _____

Date _____

STUDY QUESTIONS

1. With many aircraft, flight operations cannot be conducted safely without certain _____ electrical systems.

2. All systems and equipment installed in _____ -category aircraft must meet certain basic safety requirements, and these are set forth in FAR Part 25.

3. The _____ diagram is a type of electrical road map that identifies the various wires and electric components of a particular system.

4. Electrical schematic diagrams for light aircraft are often contained in the _____ manual.

5. The electrical schematics for larger, more complex aircraft are contained in a separate _____ diagram manual.

6. The manufacturers of corporate and transport-category aircraft typically follow the _____ specifications for categorizing data in the maintenance and wiring diagram manuals.

7. ATA specification _____ is a detailed number code of the various items found on a typical aircraft.

8. Schematics do not show _____ configurations of components within an electrical system.

9. _____ is often the term used to refer to an electric component, a communication radio, or a generator control unit.

10. The term _____ means that the component is easily removed from and installed on the aircraft.

11. The _____ zone indicates the location of each component within the aircraft.

12. Each aircraft must have three _____ lights: two forward and one aft.

13. An _____ light is designed to make the presence of an aircraft known to pilots and crew members of other aircraft in the vicinity, particularly in areas of high-density aviation activity, at night, and in conditions of reduced visibility.

14. There are two basic types of anticollision lights: _____ beacons and strobe lights.

15. Flashing-type anticollision lights are often called _____ lights.

16. _____ lights for aircraft are required to provide adequate light to illuminate the runway when the aircraft is making a landing.

17. _____ lights are installed behind the face of the instrument panel.

18. _____ lights are provided to alert the pilot and crew to operating conditions within the aircraft systems.

19. The landing-gear circuit incorporates _____ , which prevent the operation of the landing gear as long as the airplane is on the ground.

20. The flight compartment floodlights consist of two sets of _____ floodlights, one mounted in the captain's glare shield and one in the first officer's shield.

21. Fluorescent lights require a _____ transformer to increase system voltage.

22. _____ lights are located in the main and nose gear wheel wells, in electric equipment compartments, and in some engine compartments.

23. _____ compartment lights are used on most commercial aircraft to aid in the handling and storage of cargo.

24. _____ lighting circuits often include wing illumination lights, landing lights, runway turnoff lights, anticollision lights, and position lights.

25. _____ sensors are simply inductor coils that operate in conjunction with steel targets.

26. The Boeing 757 aircraft contains a _____ , which provides position sensing for landing gear, cabin doors, and thrust reversers.

27. Large aircraft often incorporate _____ systems to monitor and detect faults in a variety of aircraft systems.

28. The _____ system is used for communication between flight crew personnel and passengers.

29. An _____ system is a means of communication between flight crew members and ground service personnel.

30. The _____ is used to analyze engine parameters and power requests in order to control engine thrust, and the _____ monitors flight parameters and performs autopilot functions.

31. _____ control units monitor various electrical parameters and display system status to the flight crew.

32. On Airbus Industries aircraft a system similar to EICAS is used to monitor engine and flight parameters and is known as the _____ system.

33. During flight, aircraft produce _____ static through contact with rain, dust, snow, and other particles.

34. Precipitation static, or _____ , can also be created by the movement of jet exhaust over the aircraft's surface.

35. The 100-h, the annual, or the _____ can be used for light-aircraft inspections.

36. Large aircraft are typically maintained according to an inspection program approved by the FAA known as a _____ Airworthiness Inspection Program.

37. _____ are the simplest, where routine maintenance is performed approximately every 200 h.

38. _____ are typically complete airframe overhauls performed every 4 to 5 years.

39. _____ parts are those which deteriorate beyond use in a given length of time.

40. _____ circuits are created by broken wires, defective connectors, loose terminals, and any other condition that creates a circuit disconnection.

41. A _____ to ground from a positive wire creates an infinite current flow because of the extremely low resistance from the voltage positive to negative.

42. A _____ short occurs when two or more circuits are accidentally connected together.

43. Voltmeters are always connected in a circuit in _____ with respect to that portion of the circuit to be measured.

44. _____ are best suited for two types of tests: (a) continuity checks of components removed from a circuit and (b) continuity checks of short circuits.

45. Ohmmeters are always connected in a circuit in _____ with respect to that portion of the circuit to be measured.

46. _____ are typically used to test aircraft charging systems.

47. _____ systems found on modern commercial aircraft are designed to troubleshoot the electrical problems typically encountered during maintenance.

48. _____ are a slightly more advanced BITE system.

49. _____ effects are considered any EICAS or discrete annunciator display used to inform the flight crew of an in-flight fault.

50. The latest generation of built-in test equipment is known as the _____ .

Chapter 13

MULTIPLE-CHOICE QUESTIONS

Circle the letter of the best answer.

1. Which of the following systems is used to monitor various electrical parameters and display system status to the flight crew?
   a. EICAS
   b. BITE
   c. CMC
   d. CMDU

2. Approximately how often are large transport-category aircraft typically required to have an A-check performed during a Continuous Airworthiness Inspection Program?
   a. Every 100 flight hours
   b. Every 200 flight hours
   c. Every 300 flight hours
   d. Every 400 flight hours

3. Aircraft position lights consist of at least three lights. Their colors and locations are as follows:
   a. White in front, red in the rear, and green midway on the aircraft centerline
   b. Red on the left, green on the right, and white on the rear
   c. Green in front, red in the rear, and white midway on the aircraft centerline
   d. Red on the right, green on the left, and white in the rear

4. Aircraft that operate only ac generators (alternators) as a primary source of electric power normally provide current suitable for battery charging through the use of
   a. a stepdown transformer and rectifier.
   b. a network of condensers and choke coils to filter the alternating current with negligible power loss.
   c. an inverter and a voltage-dropping resistor.
   d. a dynamotor with a half-wave dc output.

5. Which FAR gives the general requirements for electrical systems for transport-category aircraft?
   a. Part 23
   b. Part 21
   c. Part 43
   d. Part 25

6. Flashing-type anticollision lights are called
   a. navigation lights.
   b. rotating beacons.
   c. flashing navigation beacons.
   d. strobe lights.

7. Why are aircraft components bonded?
   a. To allow electrical charges to move through the aircraft structure without causing sparks
   b. To prevent electrical charges from moving through the aircraft structure
   c. To maintain the electrostatic charge of the aircraft equal to that of the surrounding atmosphere
   d. To allow the electrostatic charge of the aircraft to dissipate before it contacts the ground after flight

8. Which instrument is used to perform continuity checks?
   a. Voltmeter
   b. Ohmmeter
   c. Ammeter
   d. Wattmeter

9. Which of the following is used to increase the voltage for a fluorescent light fixture?
   a. Rectifier
   b. Ballast transformer
   c. Ballast resistor
   d. Variable resistor

10. Where would a technician find information concerning the electrical connections of a given circuit?
    a. Schematic diagrams for that circuit
    b. The electrical manual for that aircraft
    c. The advisory circular 43.13
    d. FAR Part 23

11. Which ATA chapter covers information on electric power?
    a. 100
    b. 20
    c. 24
    d. 43

12. On the Boeing 747 where is the central maintenance computer system accessed during ground maintenance?
    a. In the electrical equipment bay
    b. In the aft cargo compartment
    c. In the forward flight attendant station
    d. On the flight deck

13. What type of fault is indicated by a red display on the CFDS of an Airbus A-320?
    a. Class 1
    b. Class 2
    c. Class 3
    d. Class 4

14. On Beechcraft electrical schematics, the location of a component is identified by which of the following?
    a. Installation zone
    b. Installation code
    c. Location zone
    d. Location code

15. If one switch is used to control all navigation lights, the lights are most likely connected
    a. in series with each other and in parallel with the switch.
    b. in series with each other and in series with the switch.
    c. in parallel with each other and in parallel with the switch.
    d. in parallel with each other and in series with the switch.

16. How many lights are needed for the position light system found on modern aircraft?
    a. 1
    b. 2
    c. 3
    d. 4

17. Static dischargers are installed on aircraft to bleed off static electricity. Elimination of static electricity is desired in order to
    a. reduce radio receiver interference.
    b. prevent opposition and surges in the aircraft's generated-power system.
    c. keep the passengers and/or the crew from experiencing static electricity shocks.
    d. prevent false indications on the aircraft's instruments.

18. In troubleshooting an electric circuit, if an ohmmeter is properly connected across a circuit component and some value of resistance is read,
    a. the component has continuity and is open.
    b. either the component or the circuit is shorted.
    c. the component has no continuity and is open.
    d. the component has continuity and is not open.

19. What color is the right position light?
    a. Red
    b. Blue
    c. White
    d. Green

20. Which of the following units are replaced by proximity sensors on many state-of-the art aircraft?
    a. Landing-gear control units
    b. Flap actuator switches
    c. Microswitches
    d. Temperature sensors

21. What is the term for an unwanted circuit disconnection?
    a. A cross short
    b. An open circuit
    c. A short to ground
    d. A completed circuit

22. In the use of a maintenance control display unit, what is meant by the term *flight deck effects?*
    a. The effect on the aircraft of an in-flight fault
    b. The action taken by the flight crew after a system failure
    c. The maintenance action required after a system failure
    d. The EICAS or annunciator display caused by a system failure

Chapter 13

Name _____

Date _____

APPLICATION QUESTIONS

1. Study the following schematic, and identify which of the groups of lights are dimmed through the use of a transistor.

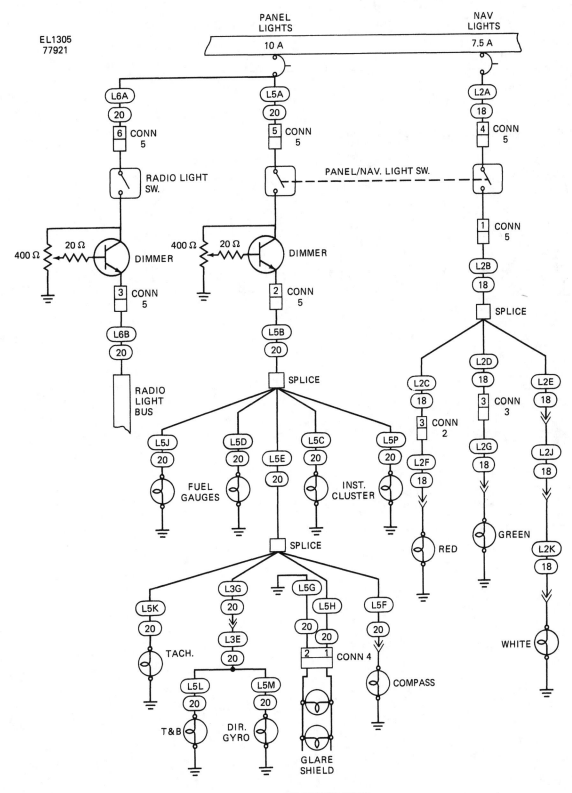

2. What values would the voltmeters indicate if connected as shown in the diagram below?

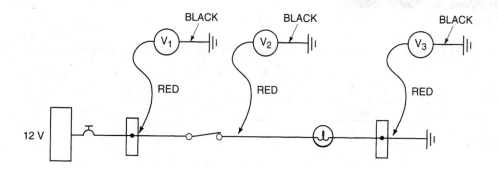

3. Which of the voltmeters in the circuit below will indicate 12 V?

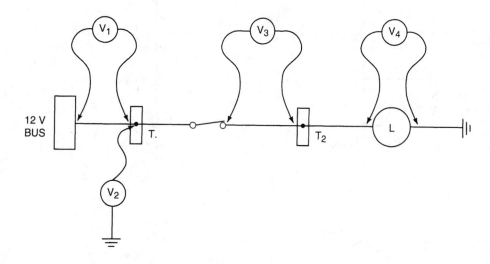

Chapter 14

Name _____

Date _____

STUDY QUESTIONS

1. Radio signals emanate from the antenna of a transmitter partly in the form of _____ waves.

2. The electromagnetic and _____ fields produced by a radio transmitter antenna are at right angles to each other.

3. The length of a radio wave depends on its _____ .

4. The _____ , indicated by the Greek letter lambda (λ), is the distance from the crest of one wave to the crest of the next.

5. The field of electric and electromagnetic energy that carries the intelligence of a radio signal is called a _____ wave.

6. Carrier waves are usually in the _____ range, which is in excess of 20,000 Hz.

7. Frequencies below 20,000 Hz are in the _____ range.

8. An RF carrier wave that has been modulated in amplitude is called an _____ signal.

9. _____ can be used in the VHF range and above and is much less affected by interference than amplitude modulation.

10. _____ waves tend to be held near the earth's surface and "bend" with the curvature of the earth.

11. _____ waves, which are produced in frequencies from 20 to 30 MHz, tend to travel in straight lines.

12. _____ waves are found in frequencies above 30 MHz, and because of their high frequencies, they can travel through the ionosphere layer of the atmosphere.

13. An _____ is a specially designed conductor that accepts energy from a transmitter and radiates it into the atmosphere.

14. Where transmitters and receivers are built into one unit, often called a _____ , the same antenna may serve for both transmitting and receiving.

15. Smaller, less efficient antennas produce less drag on the aircraft and/or can be placed behind nonconductive panels to produce a _____ antenna system.

16. The simplest types of antennas are the Hertz and the _____ , or vertical, antenna.

17. An _____ is a circuit that receives a signal of a certain amplitude and produces a signal of greater amplitude.

18. If the function of an amplifier is to amplify power or voltage, it is called a _____ amplifier or a _____ amplifier.

19. A _____ amplifier operates at a level such that the emitter-collector current flows at all times because the voltage never reaches a sufficiently negative value to cut off the electron flow.

20. A _____ amplifier is biased at approximately the cutoff point.

21. Class B amplification is often used in _____ amplifiers, in which two transistors are employed, one amplifying one half of the signal and the other amplifying the other half.

22. In _____ amplification the emitter-base circuit of the transistor is biased well beyond cutoff so that only a small portion of the positive peaks of the signal are amplified.

23. The purpose of a _____ is to convert sound energy into electric energy.

24. The _____ mic contains tiny carbon granules compressed in a sealed chamber.

25. The _____ mic uses the process of electromagnetic induction to produce the electrical signal.

26. The _____ mic uses two plates, similar to a capacitor, to produce the electric current.

27. _____ are used in radio and television transmitters to generate the RF carrier waves, in receivers to produce the intermediate frequency, and in other circuits and systems in which it is necessary to develop an alternating current with a particular frequency.

28. The purpose of the _____ amplifier is to amplify the RF signal produced by the oscillator without loading the oscillator circuit and thus causing a change in the oscillator frequency.

29. The function of the _____ , or modulation circuit, in a transmitter is to impress a signal on the RF carrier wave.

30. The function of the _____ of a transmitter is to increase the power level of the modulated signal to the point where it meets the requirements of the transmitting system.

31. An _____ is a circuit that connects the amplifier of a transmitter to its antenna.

32. In the design and operation of electronic systems, _____ circuits provide the key to frequency control.

33. Among the types of filters used in electronic circuits are high-pass filters, low-pass filters, and _____ filters.

34. A _____ filter will tend to pass high frequencies and eliminate or reduce low frequencies.

35. A _____ filter will tend to pass low frequencies and eliminate or reduce high frequencies.

36. A filter may be made from a _____ circuit by making either the inductance or the capacitance variable.

37. _____ of a radio signal is the process of separating the RF carrier wave from the AF intelligence wave.

38. Detection is often referred to as _____ because it is the opposite of the modulation process.

39. The _____ receiver is the simplest of all types of radio receivers.

40. The _____ receiver derives its name from the fact that a new signal frequency is generated in the receiver by means of a local oscillator called a beat frequency oscillator (BFO).

41. _____ tuning refers to the use of digital circuits to generate many frequencies from a single crystal oscillator.

42. The digital technique of _____ has been developed to obtain a stable tuning circuit that is capable of 0.2 MHz increments.

43. Programmable dividers, or _____ , are made from a number of flip-flop circuits in various arrangements.

Chapter 14

MULTIPLE-CHOICE QUESTIONS

Name _____

Date _____

Circle the letter of the best answer.

1. What is the range of frequencies used in various radio systems?
   a. 3 Hz to 30 MHz
   b. 3 Hz to 30 kHz
   c. 3 MHz to 30 GHz
   d. 3 kHz to 30 GHZ

2. What unit is used to produce an ac signal for radio equipment?
   a. A transistor
   b. An oscillator
   c. A modulator
   d. An amplifier

3. Which phrase below best describes a low-pass filter?
   a. An inductor in series and a capacitor in parallel
   b. A capacitor in parallel and an inductor in parallel
   c. A capacitor in parallel and in series
   d. An inductor in parallel and in series

4. Radio waves that tend to bend with the curvature of the earth are called
   a. earth waves.
   b. sky waves.
   c. gravity waves.
   d. ground waves.

5. Which type of amplifier produces a minimum amount of distortion?
   a. Class A amplifier
   b. Class B amplifier
   c. Class C amplifier
   d. Class D amplifier

6. What type of wave emanates from the antenna of a radio transmitter?
   a. Ionized radio wave
   b. Electromagnetic wave
   c. Ferromagnetic wave
   d. Induced wave

7. The distance from the crest of one radio wave to the crest of the next is called
   a. frequency.
   b. amplitude.
   c. wavelength.
   d. modulation.

8. What is the process of separating the RF carrier wave from the AF wave?
   a. Frequency modulation
   b. Amplitude modulation
   c. Demodulation
   d. Filtering

9. Which of the following is a true statement concerning space waves?
   a. Space waves are limited to line-of-sight reception.
   b. Space waves travel only where there is no atmosphere.
   c. Space waves travel best above the ionosphere.
   d. Space waves have frequencies below 30 kHz.

10. What unit is used to receive a signal of a certain amplitude and produce a signal of greater amplitude?
    a. An amplifier
    b. An antenna
    c. A modulator
    d. A demodulator

11. In a simple one-transistor radio, what does the transistor amplify?
    a. The modulated RF wave
    b. The demodulated RF wave
    c. The audio frequency wave
    d. The radio frequency wave

Chapter 14

Name _____

Date _____

APPLICATION QUESTIONS

1. Which of the following waveforms are the RF wave, the AF wave, and the modulated RF wave?

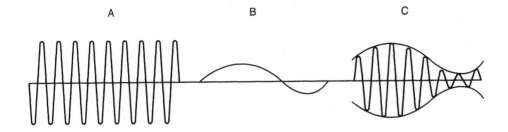

A   B   C

2. Draw a representation of amplitude modulation.

3. Draw a representation of frequency modulation.

4. Draw a diagram of a simple low-pass filter.

5. Label the sections of the radio receiver shown below.

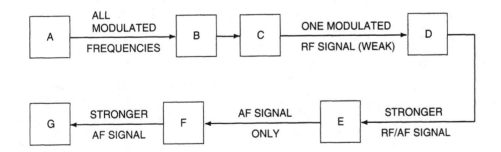

6. Determine the wavelength of a radio signal with a frequency of 120 MHz.

Chapter 15

Name _____

Date _____

STUDY QUESTIONS

1. The term _____ is a combination of the words *aviation electronics* and encompasses a variety of electronic systems.

2. All modern avionic systems conform to _____ standards.

3. The data mode is used for digital-type information that is to be linked to equipment external to the HF radio system and is known as the _____ data link.

4. The _____ is an instrument designed to relieve the pilot and copilot from continuously monitoring the aircraft radio receivers.

5. Some aircraft are equipped with _____ receivers and transmitters, which utilize orbiting communication satellites to extend their useful range.

6. It is the responsibility of the _____ to supervise all radio transmission in the United States, its territories, and its possessions.

7. The function of an _____ system is to enable the pilot to determine the heading, or direction, of each radio station being received.

8. The _____ provides visual information for the pilot and copilot concerning the data received by the ADF equipment.

9. The _____ is an electronic navigation system that enables the pilot to determine the bearings of the VOR transmitter from any position in its service area.

10. The _____ is designed to allow pilots the opportunity to land their aircraft with the aid of instrument references.

11. The ILS provides a horizontal directional reference and a vertical reference called the _____.

12. The _____ consists of two RF transmitters and an eight-loop antenna array.

13. To make it possible for a pilot to determine the distance of the aircraft from a particular VOR/DME or VORTAC station, _____ was developed.

14. In order to provide pilots with an indication of their distance from the runway, _____ transmitters are installed at fixed distances from the end of the runway.

15. The _____ has been developed to overcome some of the problems and limitations associated with the ILS.

16. The _____ controls as many as three transceivers and six receivers.

17. _____ is a system that makes it possible to use the information from VOR/DME or VORTAC stations to fly a direct route from a point of departure to a destination without following a dogleg course, which would result if NAV were used only with VOR/DME information.

18. The use of RNAV with other electronic navigation components makes possible a completely

_____ .

19. _____ is a system that operates in the LF range (30 to 300 kHz) and utilizes pulse-transmitting stations to provide the signals necessary for navigational computation.

20. The _____ utilizes worldwide stations established by the United States.

21. The advantage of an _____ is that it requires no external radio signals.

22. The instrument used to detect acceleration is called the _____ .

23. Since aircraft are seldom perfectly level during flight, all airborne accelerometers must be mounted on a

_____ .

24. A second type of INS is known as the _____ navigation system, which uses a solid-state (no moving parts) accelerometer system.

25. The _____ navigation system is so named because it utilizes the Doppler shift principle.

26. Because of the difficulty that flight controllers had in identifying aircraft on radarscopes in tower stations and control centers, radar devices called _____ were developed.

27. _____ is a transponder that provides a non-altitude-reporting, four-digit coded reply when interrogated by a ground-based ATC radar.

28. _____ is an airborne transponder that provides a coded reply identical with that of mode A; however, it also transmits an altitude-reporting signal.

29. _____ is a transponder with mode A and mode C capabilities, but it also responds to TCAS-equipped aircraft.

30. _____ works in conjunction with an aircraft's ATC transponder to inform the flight crew of aircraft that pose a potential midair collision threat.

31. Radar altimeters were developed to give an accurate indication of aircraft altitude _____ .

32. _____ are used on many commercial aircraft to warn the pilot of an excessively low aircraft altitude.

33. _____ utilize ground-based equipment that receives the transmitted signal and transfers it to a common telephone service.

34. An _____ , also referred to as a locator beacon, is required on aircraft to provide a signal or signals that will enable search aircraft or ground stations to find an aircraft that has made a crash landing in a remote or mountainous area.

35. _____ must monitor all flight compartment and communication radio conversations.

36. The _____ must monitor both flight parameters and cockpit voice activities.

37. _____ monitor the last 30 min of cockpit conversations and radio communications.

38. When a mast or a whip _____ is installed on the fuselage or any other part of an aircraft structure, it is necessary to make sure that the structure of the airplane is sufficiently strong to support the unit under all conditions of shock, vibration, or continued movement.

Chapter 15

Name _____

Date _____

MULTIPLE-CHOICE QUESTIONS

Circle the letter of the best answer.

1. What navigation radio enables the pilot to determine the headings to radio stations and operates on a frequency range of 90 to 1800 kHz?
   a. VOR
   b. NDB
   c. ILS
   d. ADF

2. How many aircraft antennas are required for the ADF radio system?
   a. 1
   b. 2
   c. 3
   d. 4

3. What is Aeronautical Radio Incorporated (ARINC)?
   a. An agency of the FAA
   b. A navigation radio manufacturer
   c. A standardization agency
   d. A data bus system manufacturer

4. What frequency group is used for air traffic control in the United States?
   a. VHF
   b. HF
   c. UHF
   d. LF

5. The purpose of a glide slope system is to
   a. provide for automatic altitude reporting to air traffic control.
   b. indicate the distance the airplane is from the end of the runway.
   c. assist the pilot in making the correct angle-of-incidence approach to the runway.
   d. assist the pilot in making a correct angle of descent to the runway.

6. What microwave band is used by SATCOM for aircraft-to-satellite transmissions?
   a. L-band
   b. C-band
   c. M-band
   d. K-band

7. Which of the following are part of the ADF systems used on aircraft?
   a. VHF transmitters
   b. UHF transmitters
   c. Marker beacons
   d. Sense and loop antennas

8. What is the relationship between the two signals radiated from a VOR ground station on the radial due north of the station?
   a. They are in phase.
   b. They are 90° out of phase.
   c. They are 180° out of phase.
   d. They are 270° out of phase.

9. How many satellites are used to form the complete Navstar global positioning system?
   a. 24
   b. 21
   c. 3
   d. 14

10. What mode of transponder is required to operate TCAS?
    a. Mode C
    b. Mode A
    c. Mode X
    d. Mode S

11. How often must a VOR receiver be tested for accuracy according to FAR Part 91?
    a. Every 120 days
    b. Every year
    c. Every 30 days
    d. Every 2 years

12. Which navigation system is used to align the aircraft with the center of the runway during landing?
    a. Glide slope
    b. VOR
    c. Localizer
    d. ADF

13. What frequency is used by the marker-beacon transmitter?
    a. 75 MHz
    b. 750 MHz
    c. 75 kHz
    d. 750 kHz

14. What is the maximum number of VHF channels available for aircraft communications?
    a. 90
    b. 360
    c. 720
    d. 760

15. In what frequency range do HF radios operate?
   a. 2 to 300 MHz
   b. 30 to 200 MHz
   c. 2 to 30 MHz
   d. 2 to 300 kHz

16. What is the maximum range of a typical VHF communication radio at an altitude of 10,000 ft?
   a. 50 mi
   b. 135 mi
   c. 315 mi
   d. 500 mi

17. What system is used to "listen" for incoming radio messages and relieve the pilot from constantly monitoring radio communications?
   a. Selcal decoder
   b. VHF decoder
   c. ACARS
   d. AIRCOM system

18. What navigation system makes it possible to fly between VOR stations without following a dogleg course?
   a. DME
   b. LOC
   c. GS
   d. RNAV

19. What unit is used in the strapdown inertial navigation system to detect aircraft motion?
   a. Doppler transmitter
   b. A radio signal frequency shift
   c. Laser gyro
   d. Phase detector

20. When coaxial cable is installed, it should be secured firmly along its entire length
   a. at 1-ft intervals.
   b. wherever the cable sags.
   c. at 2-ft intervals.
   d. at 3-ft intervals.

21. An emergency locator transmitter (ELT) battery must be capable of furnishing power for signal transmissions for at least
   a. 12 h.
   b. 24 h.
   c. 36 h.
   d. 48 h.

22. How may battery replacement for an emergency locator transmitter (ELT) be determined?
   a. By removing the batteries and testing them under a measured load to determine if 50 percent of the useful life remains.
   b. By inspection of the aircraft maintenance records to determine the installation date. ELT batteries must be replaced every 12 months.
   c. By observing the battery replacement date marked on the outside of the transmitter.
   d. By activating the transmitter and measuring the signal strength.

23. Which of the following conditions requires replacement of emergency locator transmitter (ELT) batteries?
   a. When the transmitter has a total of 30 min of operation
   b. Anytime the transmitter has operated continuously for 30 min or has a total of 45 min of operation
   c. When the batteries reach 50 percent of their useful (shelf) life as established by the manufacturer
   d. When the ambient temperature has risen to 110° F (43° C) for 6 or more h

1. Label the antennas for a typical light twin-engine aircraft as shown in the diagram below.

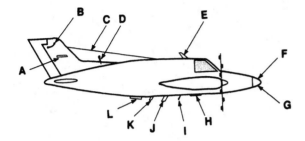

2. Determine the length of a Hertz antenna for a radio that operates at 20 MHz.

3. Determine the length of a ¼-wavelength antenna for a radio that operates at a frequency of 130 MHz.

Chapter 16

Name _____

Date _____

STUDY QUESTIONS

1. A system developed to determine weather conditions well ahead of an airplane is called a

   _____ system.

2. The word *radar* is derived from the expression _____ .

3. The _____ provides the timing for the radar signal and synchronizes the transmitter, receiver, and indicator so that all operate together with correct timing.

4. The _____ stores energy and supplies high-voltage pulses that are released by the trigger pulse from the synchronizer.

5. When the trigger pulse releases this energy, a high-voltage pulse is delivered to the _____ .

6. The principal element of a radar transmitter is a _____ tube.

7. The magnetron makes use of _____ to generate the correct frequency for the transmitted pulse.

8. The _____ is an electronic switching device that alternately connects the transmitter and receiver to the antenna.

9. The _____ can be compared to a searchlight that rotates to search a particular area with a light beam.

10. In a radar system the RF energy pulses travel along the waveguide, which terminates in a

    _____ .

11. A _____ is a hollow metallic tube, typically rectangular, used to direct the high-frequency radar waves to and from the antenna.

12. The _____ of a radar system defines its ability to accurately display the various levels of storm activity scanned by the radar.

13. The _____ is used to establish the range of the indicator.

14. The _____ is used to adjust the IF receiver gain to the proper operating point to assure reception of even the weakest reflected signals.

15. When the _____ is turned on, the transmitted radar signal will scan parallel to the earth regardless of the pitch and roll of the aircraft.

16. The _____ is used to change the angle in which the antenna is scanning.

17. Most modern radar systems employ a _____ radar antenna.

18. The radar antenna is typically mounted in the nose section of the airplane and protected by a nonmetallic, streamlined

    cover called a _____ .

19. _____ strips may also be used to help discharge any static accumulation on the radome.

20. The _____ system actually measures storm turbulence and indicates its presence with the color magenta on the radar display.

Chapter 16

Name _____

Date _____

MULTIPLE-CHOICE QUESTIONS

Circle the letter of the best answer.

1. What is used for the display of a common weather radar?
   a. An LED
   b. An LCD
   c. A CRT
   d. An AMT

2. A typical weather mapping system displays the storm activity as which of the following?
   a. A color display on a CRT
   b. A black-and-white picture on a CRT
   c. A cluster of dots forming a picture on an LCD
   d. A cluster of dots on a CRT

3. What unit is used to protect an antenna system from rain, dirt, and other elements?
   a. A radome
   b. A waveguide
   c. A phased-array plate
   d. A duplexer

4. What unit is used to carry the high-energy radar signal to the radar antenna?
   a. Waveguide
   b. Duplexer
   c. Magnetron
   d. Coaxial cable

5. What is the value of the intermediate frequency produced by the receiver section of the weather radar as it converts the incoming RF wave?
   a. 60 MHz
   b. 5400 MHz
   c. 60 Hz
   d. 5400 kHz

6. Which of the following is true concerning X-band radar?
   a. X-band is used for air-traffic-control radar.
   b. X-band has a poor resolution for weather radar.
   c. X-band is in the frequency range of 4000 to 8000 MHz.
   d. X-band radar does not provide reliable coverage behind precipitation.

7. The pulse system used for radar energy transmission allows the unit to have a relatively low input power of approximately 10 W, while the radar pulse is approximately
   a. 250 W.
   b. 25,000 W.
   c. 100 W.
   d. 10,000 W.

8. Which unit provides coordination of the various radar units to ensure correct timing of the various systems?
   a. Mixer
   b. Magnetron
   c. Synchronizer
   d. Duplexer

9. What does the receiver of a Doppler radar measure to detect wind shear?
   a. The amplitude of the reflected signal
   b. The modulation of the returned signal
   c. The frequency of the returned signal
   d. The wavelength of the returned signal

10. Static discharge damage on a radome will typically appear as which of the following?
    a. Carbon traces on the radome
    b. Cracks in the radome
    c. Moisture trapped in the radome laminae
    d. Corrosion on the radome fasteners

11. Which of the following is not a color used to indicate one of the three levels of storm activity on a typical color weather radar?
    a. Green
    b. Blue
    c. Yellow
    d. Red

Chapter 16

Name _____

Date _____

APPLICATION QUESTIONS

1. Identify the sections of a basic weather radar in the block diagram below.

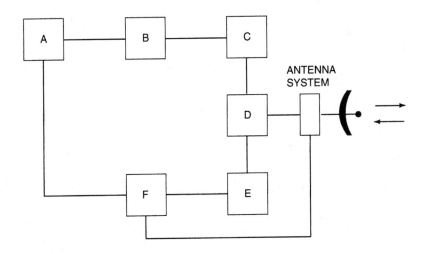

2. Draw the radiation patterns of the radar signals from (*a*) a flat-plate antenna and (*b*) a parabolic antenna.

3. Label the diagram below to show the distance from an operating radar antenna that will provide safe exposure for humans.

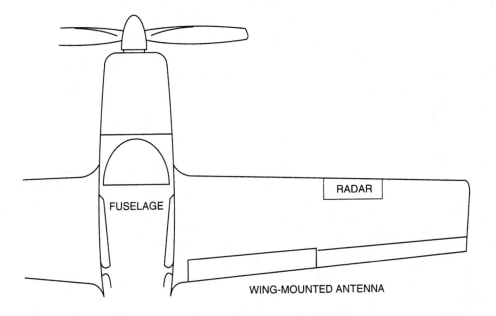

Chapter 17

Name _____

Date _____

STUDY QUESTIONS

1. A _____ is used to show the rpm of reciprocating engines, the percentage of power for turbine engines, the rpm of helicopter rotors, and the rotational speed of any other device where this information is critical.

2. _____ temperature indicators are used most frequently when it is necessary to measure comparatively high temperatures.

3. A _____ system is designed to measure an angular deflection at one point and reproduce this same deflection at a remote point.

4. Synchros have been designed and built under a variety of names, the most common being (a General Electric trade name) and _____ (a Bendix trade name).

5. Electric fuel-quantity indicators utilize a _____ resistor in the tank unit or sensor.

6. Electronic fuel indicators utilize a variable _____ as the sensor unit in the fuel tank.

7. A system that provides fuel-flow and fuel-quantity indications is called a _____ .

8. Typically, the ADI and HSI work in conjunction with the _____ system.

9. _____ are another type of hybrid electromechanical instrument package.

10. In a further attempt to reduce pilot workload and instrument panel clutter, the _____ was developed.

11. The _____ receives input signals from several aircraft and engine sensors, processes this information, and sends it to the appropriate display.

12. The _____ is an electrically driven gyro unit that provides a visual indication of the rate of turn and at the same time provides an electric signal for the autopilot with the same information.

13. The _____ is an attitude indicator and an attitude sensor.

14. The _____ is used to activate an elevator trim tab control to relieve long-term aerodynamic loading and generally assist in smoother operation of the elevator surface without requiring large amounts of power from the primary servo.

15. The _____ provides an airspeed autothrottle mode and an angle-of-attack autothrottle mode.

16. The positions of flight control surfaces must be known to the pilots, and these positions are displayed by means of the _____ .

17. A _____ detects opens and jams in the pitch-axis control system and jams in the roll-axis control system and displays to pilots the means for alleviating these problems.

18. The _____ automatically restricts the rudder authority and limits rudder hydraulic power capability during high-speed flight.

19. The _____ automatically changes the configuration of the roll and speedbrake inputs to the spoilers to optimize roll, direct lift control, and speedbrake control characteristics.

20. The _____ artificially vibrates the control columns to warn of an impending stall.

21. The _____ permits electrical control of pitch-axis trim by the pilots through the use of thumbwheels on the control wheels.

22. The _____ automatically adjusts the pitch-axis feel-force gradient for all flight conditions.

23. The _____ is a means of alleviating mechanical jams in the pitch trim system.

24. The _____ uses visual and aural warnings to indicate approaches to and deviations from selected altitudes.

25. The term _____ refers to the use of ring laser rate sensors for aircraft inertial navigation and flight reference systems.

26. The _____ is a computer-based flight control system.

Chapter 17

MULTIPLE-CHOICE QUESTIONS

Name _____

Date _____

Circle the letter of the best answer.

1. What is the primary purpose of an autopilot?
   a. To relieve the pilot of control of the aircraft during long periods of flight
   b. To provide a secondary system of aircraft guidance
   c. To fly a more precise course for the pilot
   d. To obtain the navigational aid necessary for extended flights over water

2. The rotor in an Autosyn remote indicating system uses
   a. an electromagnet.
   b. a permanent magnet.
   c. an electromagnet and a permanent magnet.
   d. neither an electromagnet nor a permanent magnet.

3. What type of electromechanical instrument incorporates command bars as part of its display?
   a. The horizontal situation indicator
   b. The air data display
   c. The symbol generator
   d. The attitude director indicator

4. What system is found on many modern transport-category aircraft to replace most of the electromechanical instruments?
   a. An electronic flight instrument system
   b. A computerized flight management system
   c. An analog flight director system
   d. A digital flight director system

5. In a dc tachometer system, the voltage output is a function of which of the following?
   a. The rotational speed of the permanent magnet
   b. The strength of the electromagnetic field
   c. The number of windings in the armature circuit
   d. The number of windings in the electromagnet

6. A common ac tachometer uses what kind of stator?
   a. Single-phase
   b. Two-phase
   c. Three-phase
   d. Four-phase

7. What is measured by the ring laser gyro to detect angular displacement of the aircraft?
   a. The amplitude of a single laser beam
   b. The amplitude of two laser beams
   c. The frequency of a single laser beam
   d. The frequency of two laser beams

8. How many flight management computers are employed by the flight management system of a Boeing 757?
   a. 1
   b. 2
   c. 3
   d. 4

9. Thermocouple leads are often made of what materials?
   a. Constantan and iron
   b. Iron and copper
   c. Copper and zinc
   d. Lead and zinc

10. What type of instrument is commonly used to measure temperatures below 300°F [148.9°C]?
    a. A thermocouple instrument
    b. A Wheatstone bridge instrument
    c. A magnesian instrument
    d. An Autosyn instrument

11. Which of the following are two common fuel-quantity indicators?
    a. Resistance and transducer types
    b. Resistance and capacitance types
    c. Capacitance and transducer types
    d. Capacitance and inductance types

12. What is the main purpose of a servomotor in an autopilot system?
    a. To correct for displacement of the aircraft about its axis
    b. To change mechanical energy to electric energy
    c. To move the control surface as commanded
    d. To drive the control surface back to the streamlined position

13. The basic difference between an Autosyn and a magnesian indicating system is the
    a. rotor.
    b. transmitter.
    c. receiver.
    d. winding.

14. The rotor in a magnesian remote indicating system uses
    a. a permanent magnet.
    b. an electromagnet.
    c. an electromagnet and a permanent magnet.
    d. neither an electromagnet nor a permanent magnet.

15. Which alert message of the EICAS requires immediate attention?
    a. Level A
    b. Level B
    c. Level C
    d. Level D

16. Where is the multifunction display of a typical EFIS located?
    a. On the left side of the instrument panel
    b. In the center of the instrument panel
    c. On the right side of the instrument panel
    d. In the electronic equipment rack

17. On many modern aircraft, what two systems indicate airframe and power plant parameters?
    a. The EADI and EHSI
    b. The ADI and HSI
    c. The EICAS and MPU
    d. The EICAS and ECAM

Chapter 17

Name _____

Date _____

APPLICATION QUESTIONS

1. For the bridge circuit below, determine the voltage measured by V_1 if the variable resistor (R_3) is 40 Ω.

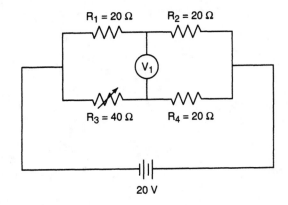

$R_1 = 20\ \Omega$ $R_2 = 20\ \Omega$

V_1

$R_3 = 40\ \Omega$ $R_4 = 20\ \Omega$

20 V

2. Label the items marked by arrows on the HSI display below.

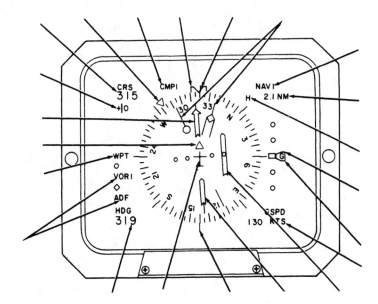

3. Label the items marked by arrows on the ADI display below.

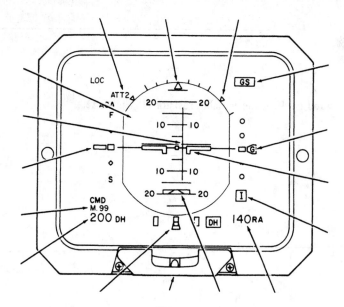

Answers

Chapter 1
STUDY QUESTIONS

1. Electronics
2. electron theory
3. molecule
4. atom
5. element
6. compound
7. nucleus
8. positive / negative
9. neutral / positively
10. negatively
11. positive ion / negative ion
12. conductors
13. free electrons
14. valence orbit
15. valence electrons
16. insulators
17. semiconductors
18. hole
19. electrostatics
20. static / static electricity
21. electrostatic force
22. current
23. ampere
24. I
25. amps
26. electromotive force
27. volt
28. volt
29. voltage
30. E / V
31. Resistance
32. ohm
33. R
34. Insulators
35. magnet
36. north / south
37. permanent magnet
38. natural magnet / lodestone
39. magnetic variation
40. Residual
41. permanent magnet
42. permeability
43. high
44. low
45. temporary
46. permanent
47. magnetic field
48. magnetic flux
49. magnetic circuit
50. reluctance
51. rel
52. Electromagnets
53. solenoid
54. relays
55. low-current
56. armature
57. static electricity
58. Piezoelectricity
59. photoelectric effect
60. thermoelectric effect
61. thermocouple
62. Chemical action
63. Electromagnetic induction
64. induction
65. electromagnetic induction
66. generator action / transformer action

Chapter 1
MULTIPLE-CHOICE QUESTIONS

1. c
2. b
3. b
4. b
5. d
6. a
7. a
8. b
9. b
10. b

Chapter 1
APPLICATION QUESTIONS

1.

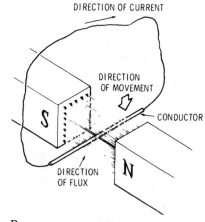

2.

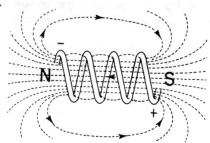

3. B

Chapter 2
STUDY QUESTIONS

1. Ohm's law
2. E
3. R / I
4. intensity
5. directly / inversely
6. volt
7. $I = E/R$
8. doubled
9. doubled / one-half
10. work
11. watt
12. IR loss
13. joule
14. potential
15. battery
16. negative / positive
17. ground
18. series
19. parallel
20. series-parallel
21. directly
22. divides
23. resistance
24. reciprocal
25. series
26. parallel

Chapter 2
MULTIPLE-CHOICE QUESTIONS

1. d
2. d
3. d
4. d
5. b
6. b
7. a
8. a
9. b
10. c
11. c
12. c
13. a
14. c
15. c
16. a
17. c
18. d

Chapter 2
APPLICATION QUESTIONS

1. $V_6 = 2.51$ V / I = 0.0023A / $R_T = 11{,}962.16$ Ω
2. I = 0.00175 A / $V_1 = 7$ V / $V_2 = 3.5$ V / $V_3 = 17.5$ V
3. 1400 W
4. $I = 0.4$ A
5. $I = 34$ A
6. $P = 0.084$ W
7. $I_T = 0.044$ A / $R_T = 634$ Ω
8. $P = 320$ W
9. $I_T = 0.089$ A / $R_T = 313$ Ω

Chapter 3
STUDY QUESTIONS

1. dc
2. electrolyte
3. cell
4. ion
5. dry cell
6. 2.1 V
7. secondary
8. primary
9. alkaline
10. Sintering
11. open-circuit voltage
12. closed-circuit voltage
13. internal resistance
14. greater
15. storage
16. vented cell / sealed (recombinant gas)
17. engine starting
18. emergency
19. 30
20. lead peroxide (PbO_2)

21. lead (Pb)
22. sulfuric acid / water
23. grid
24. terminal post
25. plate strap
26. separators
27. more rapidly
28. freeze
29. safety glasses
30. negative
31. short circuit
32. open flame
33. discharged
34. manufacturer's maintenance instructions
35. hydrometer
36. specific gravity
37. decreases
38. current / voltage
39. well-ventilated area
40. disconnecting
41. charging
42. electrolyte
43. power-to-weight
44. Thermal runaway
45. deep-cycled
46. Capacity
47. milliampere-hours (mAh)
48. ampere-hours

Chapter 3
MULTIPLE-CHOICE QUESTIONS

1. c
2. c
3. a
4. a
5. b
6. d
7. d
8. a
9. d
10. c
11. d
12. b
13. a
14. c
15. a
16. c
17. a
18. c
19. b

Chapter 3
APPLICATION QUESTIONS

1. $E_T = 55.5$ V
2. $E_T = 15$ V / $I_T = 20$ A

3.

	CHARGED STATE	CHEMICAL CHARGE	DISCHARGE
POSITIVE PLATE	PbO_2	LOSES O_2 GAINS SO_4	$PbSO_4$
NEGATIVE PLATE	Pb	GAINS SO_4	$PbSO_4$
ELECTROLYTE	H_2SO_4	LOSES SO_4 GAINS O_2	H_2O

Chapter 4
STUDY QUESTIONS

1. wire
2. cable
3. shielded
4. coaxial cable
5. antenna
6. heat
7. American Wire Gage (AWG)
8. circular mil
9. square mil
10. current
11. voltage drop
12. continuous
13. Intermittent
14. data bus cable
15. open wiring
16. flexible
17. not acceptable
18. Soldered terminals
19. Denatured alcohol
20. splicing
21. splicing connector
22. Solder splices
23. heat shrink
24. insulation
25. electrolytic
26. line replaceable units (LRUs)
27. connector assembly
28. sockets / pins
29. terminal block module
30. potting
31. Bonding
32. bonding jumper
33. Shielding
34. Electromagnetic interference
35. electromagnetic compatibility
36. HERF
37. wire identification number
38. wire bundle code
39. schematics

Chapter 4
MULTIPLE-CHOICE QUESTIONS

1. a
2. b
3. c
4. a
5. d
6. c
7. b
8. a
9. c
10. b
11. b
12. d
13. c
14. c
15. b
16. c
17. a

Chapter 4
APPLICATION QUESTIONS

1. 14 gage
2. 4 gage
3. 6 gage

Chapter 5
STUDY QUESTIONS

1. Alternating
2. sine wave
3. frequency / hertz
4. alternation
5. phase
6. phase angle
7. polyphase circuits
8. Capacitance
9. capacitor
10. lead
11. capacitive reactance
12. inversely
13. inductance
14. inductive reactance
15. proportional
16. resistive circuit
17. capacitive
18. impedance
19. True power
20. Apparent power
21. Reactive power
22. watts (W) / voltamperes (VA) / voltamperes-reactive (VAR)
23. Power factor
24. three-phase
25. transformer
26. inverter

Chapter 5
MULTIPLE-CHOICE QUESTIONS

1. d
2. b
3. d
4. a
5. d
6. a
7. d
8. d
9. d
10. b
11. c
12. d
13. b

Chapter 5
APPLICATION QUESTIONS

1. V_{RMS} = 3.5 V
2. Frequency = 2 Hz
3. C_T = 22 F
4. C_T = 1.5 F
5. X_C = 2.69 Ω
6. X_L = 25,120 Ω
7. Z = 5022.01 Ω

Chapter 6
STUDY QUESTIONS

1. switch
2. solenoids
3. derating factor
4. open / closed
5. normally open
6. close
7. normally closed
8. duty cycle
9. intermittent
10. continuous
11. Proximity sensors
12. short circuit
13. fuse
14. circuit breaker
15. Thermal
16. resistor
17. ohms / watts
18. adjustable resistor
19. variable resistor
20. rheostat
21. three
22. Voltage dividers
23. capacitor
24. dielectric
25. capacitance
26. plates
27. variable

28. electrolytic
29. electrolyte
30. Inductance
31. number of turns
32. transformer
33. primary / secondary
34. eddy currents
35. step-up
36. step-down
37. rectifier
38. solid-state
39. silicon
40. cathode
41. anode
42. diode
43. forward-biased
44. reverse-biased
45. half-wave rectification
46. transistor
47. switching transistor
48. Amplification
49. gain
50. thyristor
51. zener
52. Photodiodes
53. Thermistors
54. printed circuit boards

Chapter 6
MULTIPLE-CHOICE QUESTIONS

1. c
2. d
3. a
4. c
5. a
6. a
7. c
8. c
9. a
10. a
11. d
12. d
13. c
14. d

Chapter 6
APPLICATION QUESTIONS

1. $I = 30$ A
2. a. single pole, double throw
   b. double pole, single throw
3. a. 15-A circuit breaker
   b. 20-A fuse
4. potentiometer
5. $E = 345$ V / $I = 3.3$ A
6. series

7.

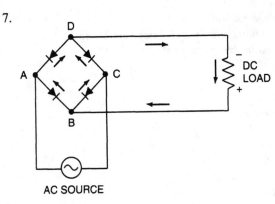

AC SOURCE

8. a. *npn*
   b.

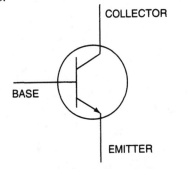

NPN Transistor

9. position A

Chapter 7
STUDY QUESTIONS

1. digital
2. analog
3. Logic circuits
4. binary
5. bit
6. byte
7. word
8. binary-coded
9. octal
10. hexadecimal
11. Logic
12. Truth
13. AND
14. OR
15. INVERT
16. NOT
17. NOR
18. NAND
19. exclusive OR
20. positive
21. negative
22. voltage-waveform
23. integrated
24. Photolithography
25. logic families
26. CMOS

27. transistor-transistor
28. complimentary metal-oxide semiconductor
29. dual in-line package (DIP)
30. Surface
31. DIP
32. Adders
33. Subtracter
34. digital
35. crystal
36. Latches
37. Microprocessors
38. Multichip
39. central processing unit (CPU)
40. CPU
41. ALU
42. memory
43. permanent
44. temporary
45. data bus
46. synchronizer
47. initialization routine
48. Subroutines
49. address
50. control bus
51. Peripherals
52. central processing unit (CPU)
53. arithmetic logic unit (ALU)
54. control
55. data transfer
56. volatile
57. nonvolatile
58. volatile memory
59. read-only memory (ROM)
60. Random-access
61. read-only
62. EAROM (electronically alterable read-only memory)
63. serial
64. Parallel data
65. multiplexers (MUXes)
66. data transfer
67. Aeronautical Radio Incorporated (ARINC)
68. ARINC 429
69. bidirectional
70. CSDB (commercial standard digital bus)
71. ASCB (avionics standard communication bus)
72. logic
73. detection / isolation
74. central maintenance computer system (CMCS)
75. data bus analyzer
76. logic probe
77. logic monitor
78. High-energy electromagnetic fields (HERFs)
79. ESDS (electrostatic-discharge-sensitive)

Chapter 7
MULTIPLE-CHOICE QUESTIONS

1. c
2. a
3. b
4. d
5. a
6. a
7. a
8. d
9. c
10. d
11. a
12. a
13. b
14. d

Chapter 7
APPLICATION QUESTIONS

1. output = 1
2.

A	B	C
0	0	0
0	1	1
1	0	1
1	1	1

An OR Gate Truth Table

3. output = 0
4. output = 1
5. a NAND gate
6. parity bit = 1
7. 291 kn

Chapter 8
STUDY QUESTIONS

1. wattmeter
2. galvanometer
3. d'Arsonval
4. dynamometer
5. iron vane
6. taut-band movement
7. Sensitivity
8. shunt resistor
9. instrument shunt
10. shunt
11. voltmeter
12. multipliers
13. ohmmeter
14. continuity
15. hot-wire
16. rectifier
17. inductive pickup
18. Frequency

19. multimeter
20. Hall-effect
21. oscilloscope
22. transducers

Chapter 8
MULTIPLE-CHOICE QUESTIONS

1. b
2. d
3. a
4. c
5. a
6. c
7. b
8. a

Chapter 8
APPLICATION QUESTIONS

1. Total amperage of the circuit
2. The voltage over R_1
3. The lamp must be isolated from the power source before a continuity test is performed.

Chapter 9
STUDY QUESTIONS

1. electric
2. compound-wound
3. electromagnetic
4. right-hand motor rule
5. constant-speed
6. reversible
7. slip clutch
8. limit
9. thermal
10. synchronous
11. universal
12. slip
13. pull-out
14. capacitor
15. repulsion
16. Synchronous
17. friction
18. windage
19. copper
20. eddy current
21. Hysteresis losses
22. three-phase induction

Chapter 9
MULTIPLE-CHOICE QUESTIONS

1. b
2. c
3. d
4. c

5. c
6. a
7. c
8. c
9. b
10. c
11. b
12. a
13. c
14. a
15. b
16. a

Chapter 9
APPLICATION QUESTIONS

1.

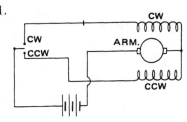

2.

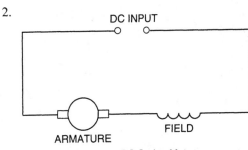

A Simple DC Series Motor

3. a. brush set
   b. commutator
   c. armature
   d. frame and field assembly
   e. bendix drive

Chapter 10
STUDY QUESTIONS

1. electric
2. electromagnetic
3. left-hand
4. magnetic
5. armature
6. brushes
7. field poles
8. field coils
9. speed
10. commutator
11. commutation
12. residual
13. compound-wound
14. cross magnetization

15. armature reaction
16. interpoles
17. compensating winding
18. field housing
19. end frames
20. Starter-generators
21. shear section
22. speed / conductors / strength
23. reverse-current cutout
24. current-limiting
25. three-unit control panel
26. generator control unit
27. paralleling
28. wear groove
29. Instant filming

d. blast tube
e. woodruff key
f. drive end frame
g. field coils
h. armature
i. pole shoes
j. cover band
k. commutator end frame
l. brush
4. a. charge 2 A
   b. discharge 20 A

Chapter 10
MULTIPLE-CHOICE QUESTIONS

1. c
2. c
3. d
4. a
5. d
6. c
7. d
8. c
9. c
10. c
11. c
12. d
13. a
14. a
15. c

Chapter 10
APPLICATION QUESTIONS

1.

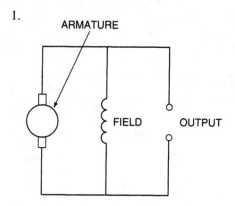

ARMATURE

FIELD   OUTPUT

A Simple Shunt-Wound Generator

2. a. voltage coil
   b. current coil
   c. current coil
3. a. bearing
   b. terminals
   c. commutator

Chapter 11
STUDY QUESTIONS

1. ac
2. Electromagnetic
3. rotating field
4. regulator
5. rotor
6. three-phase, full-wave rectifier
7. slip rings
8. transistorized
9. alternator control unit
10. ram air turbines (RATs)
11. frequency
12. High-output brushless
13. constant-speed drive (CSD)
14. quick attach/detach (QAD)
15. integrated drive generator (IDG)
16. generator control unit (GCU)
17. bus power control unit (BPCU)
18. inverter
19. static
20. Variable-speed constant-frequency systems

Chapter 11
MULTIPLE-CHOICE QUESTIONS

1. b
2. c
3. b
4. b
5. a
6. b
7. b
8. b
9. d
10. d
11. c
12. a
13. c
14. d
15. a
16. a
17. d
18. c

Chapter 11
APPLICATION QUESTION

1. a. drive end housing
   b. cooling fan
   c. rotor (field coil)
   d. slip rings
   e. stator (armature assembly)
   f. rectifiers
   g. brush end housing
   h. brush assembly

Chapter 12
STUDY QUESTIONS

1. bus bar
2. ground / negative
3. airframe
4. single
5. Part 23
6. Part 25
7. load analysis
8. 5
9. 30
10. trip-free
11. 50 percent
12. essential
13. master
14. continuous
15. Intermittent
16. probable
17. ammeter
18. "red-lined"
19. electrical-load analysis
20. voltage spike
21. ground plane
22. direct / indirect
23. bonding jumpers
24. split bus / parallel
25. parallel
26. synchronizing
27. load
28. hierarchy
29. shedding
30. controllers
31. no-break

Chapter 12
MULTIPLE-CHOICE QUESTIONS

1. d
2. c
3. a
4. c
5. d
6. a
7. d
8. b
9. d
10. a
11. b
12. a

Chapter 12
APPLICATION QUESTIONS

1. No
2. The isolation limiters are high-amperage fuses used to disconnect the right or left generator bus from the isolation bus in the event of an extreme current flow condition.
3. The No. 1 dual feed bus
4. The dashed lines represent various interlock switches and relays.
5. Parallel
6. GB 2 (generator breaker 2) and BTB 2 (bus tie breaker 2)

Chapter 13
STUDY QUESTIONS

1. essential
2. transport
3. schematic
4. maintenance
5. wiring
6. Air Transport Association (ATA)
7. 100
8. physical
9. Black box
10. line replaceable unit (LRU)
11. installation
12. position
13. anticollision
14. rotating
15. strobe
16. Landing
17. Instrument
18. Warning
19. landing-gear safety switches ("squat" switches)
20. fluorescent
21. ballast
22. Service
23. Cargo
24. Exterior
25. Proximity
26. proximity switch electronic unit (PSEU)
27. built-in test equipment (BITE)
28. intercom
29. interphone
30. thrust management computer (TMC) / flight management computer (FMC)
31. Engine indicating and crew alerting system (EICAS)
32. electronic centralized aircraft monitoring (ECAM)
33. precipitation

34. P-static
35. periodic inspection program
36. Continuous
37. A-checks
38. D-checks
39. Life-limited
40. Open
41. short
42. cross
43. parallel
44. Ohmmeters
45. series
46. Ammeters
47. Built-in test equipment (BITE)
48. Maintenance control display units (MCDUs)
49. Flight deck
50. central maintenance computer system (CMCS)

Chapter 13
MULTIPLE-CHOICE QUESTIONS

1. a
2. b
3. b
4. a
5. d
6. d
7. a
8. b
9. b
10. a
11. c
12. d
13. a
14. a
15. d
16. c
17. a
18. d
19. d
20. c
21. b
22. d

Chapter 13
APPLICATION QUESTIONS

1. The panel lights and the radio lights are dimmed through the use of a transistor circuit.
2. $V_1 = 12$ V; $V_2 = 12$ V; $V_3 = 0$ V
3. Voltmeters V_2 and V_4 will both indicate 12 V.

Chapter 14
STUDY QUESTIONS

1. electromagnetic
2. electric

3. frequency
4. wavelength
5. carrier
6. radio frequency (RF)
7. audio frequency (AF)
8. amplitude-modulated (AM)
9. Frequency modulation (FM)
10. Ground
11. Sky
12. Space
13. antenna
14. transceiver
15. flush-mounted
16. Marconi
17. amplifier
18. power / voltage
19. class A
20. class B
21. push-pull
22. class C
23. microphone (mic)
24. carbon
25. dynamic
26. electret
27. Oscillators
28. buffer
29. modulator
30. power amplifier
31. antenna coupler
32. resonant
33. band-pass
34. high-pass
35. low-pass
36. tuning
37. Detection
38. demodulation
39. crystal
40. superheterodyne
41. Digital
42. frequency synthesis
43. counters

Chapter 14
MULTIPLE-CHOICE QUESTIONS

1. d
2. b
3. a
4. d
5. a
6. b
7. c
8. c
9. a
10. a
11. c

Chapter 14
APPLICATION QUESTIONS

1. a. the RF carrier wave
   b. the AF wave
   c. the modulated RF wave

2.

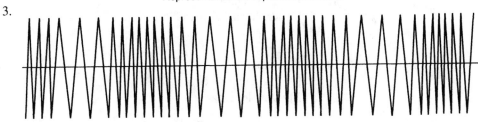

Representation of Amplified Modulation

3.

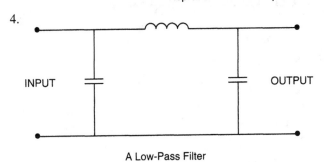

Representation of Frequence Modulation

4.

INPUT   OUTPUT

A Low-Pass Filter

5. a. antenna
   b. antenna coupler
   c. tuner
   d. preamplifier;
   e. demodulator
   f. power amplifier
   g. speaker
6. 2.5 ft

Chapter 15
STUDY QUESTIONS

1. avionics
2. Aeronautical Radio Incorporated (ARINC)
3. air-ground
4. Selcal decoder
5. satellite communication (SATCOM)
6. Federal Communications Commission (FCC)
7. automatic direction-finder (ADF)
8. radio magnetic indicator (RMI)
9. VHF Omnirange (VOR)

10. instrument landing system (ILS)
11. glide slope
12. localizer
13. distance-measuring equipment (DME)
14. marker-beacon
15. microwave landing system (MLS)
16. audio control system
17. Area navigation (RNAV)
18. integrated navigation system
19. LORAN (LOng-RAnge Navigation)
20. VLF/OMEGA navigation system
21. inertial navigation system (INS)
22. accelerometer
23. gimbal platform
24. strapdown inertial
25. Doppler
26. ATC (air traffic control) transponders
27. Mode A
28. Mode C
29. Mode S

30. TCAS (traffic alert and collision avoidance system)
31. above ground level (AGL)
32. Ground proximity warning systems (GPWs)
33. Radio telephones
34. emergency locator transmitter (ELT)
35. Voice recorders
36. flight data recording system
37. Cockpit voice recorders (CVRs)
38. antenna

Chapter 15
MULTIPLE-CHOICE QUESTIONS

1. d
2. b
3. c
4. a
5. d
6. a
7. d
8. a
9. a
10. d
11. c
12. c
13. a
14. d
15. c
16. b
17. a
18. d
19. c
20. c
21. d
22. c
23. c

Chapter 15
APPLICATION QUESTIONS

1. a. RNAV
   b. VOR, localizer
   c. ADF sense
   d. ELT
   e. VHF com
   f. glide slope
   g. radar
   h. marker beacon
   i. transponder
   j. VHF com
   k. DME
   l. ADF loop
2. 24.6 ft
3. 1.8 ft

Chapter 16
STUDY QUESTIONS

1. weather mapping
2. radio detecting and ranging
3. synchronizer
4. mixer
5. transmitter
6. magnetron
7. resonant cavities
8. duplexer
9. antenna system
10. feed element
11. waveguide
12. resolution
13. range control
14. gain control
15. stabilization control
16. tilt control
17. flat-plate
18. radome
19. Lightning diverter
20. Doppler radar

Chapter 16
MULTIPLE-CHOICE QUESTIONS

1. c
2. d
3. a
4. a
5. a
6. d
7. b
8. c
9. c
10. a
11. b

Chapter 16
APPLICATION QUESTIONS

1. a. synchronizer
   b. modulator
   c. transmitter
   d. duplexer
   e. receiver
   f. indicator

2.

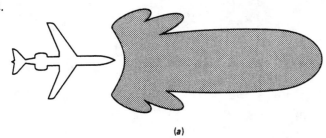

(a)

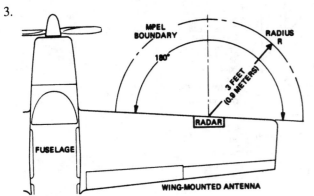

SIGNAL LOSS

(b)

3.

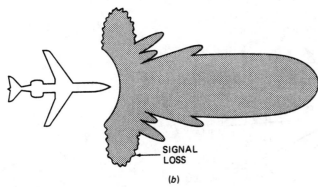

Chapter 17
STUDY QUESTIONS

1. tachometer
2. Thermocouple
3. synchro
4. Selsyn / Autosyn
5. variable
6. capacitor
7. computerized fuel system (CFS)
8. flight director
9. Air data systems
10. electronic flight instrument system (EFIS)
11. symbol generator (SG)
12. turn-and-bank indicator
13. director horizon indicator (DHI)
14. trim servo
15. speed control system (SCS)
16. surface position indicator
17. primary flight control monitoring system (PFCMS)
18. rudder-control limiting system
19. spoiler mode-control system
20. stall warning system
21. electric pitch trim system
22. Mach feel system
23. pitch trim disconnect system
24. altitude alert system
25. strapdown technology
26. flight management system (FMS)

Chapter 17
MULTIPLE-CHOICE QUESTIONS

1. a
2. a
3. d
4. a
5. a
6. c
7. d
8. b
9. a

10. b
11. b
12. c
13. a
14. a
15. a
16. b
17. d

Chapter 17
APPLICATION QUESTIONS

1. $E = 3.4$ V
2.

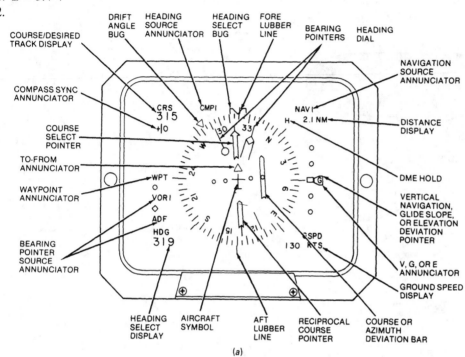

(a)

3.

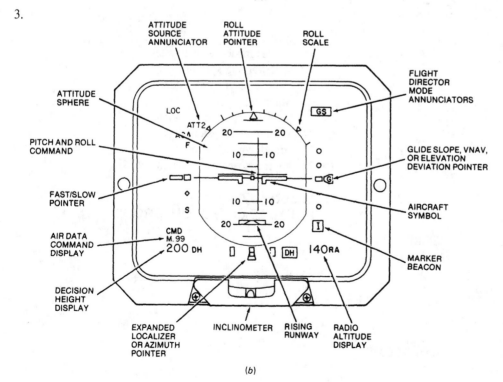

(b)

Study Guide for Aircraft Electricity and Electronics